Power Plyometrics

POWER PLYOMETRICS

THE COMPLETE PROGRAM

Ed McNeely, David Sandler

Meyer & Meyer Sport

British Library Cataloguing in Publication Data
A catalogue record for this book is available from the British Library

Power Plyometrics
Maidenhead: Meyer & Meyer Sport (UK) Ltd., 2007
ISBN: 978-1-84126-200-0

2nd edition 2009
Aachen, Adelaide, Auckland, Budapest, Cape Town, Graz,
Indianapolis, Maidenhead, Olten (CH), Singapore, Toronto
Member of the World
Sports Publishers' Association (WSPA)
www.w-s-p-a.org
Printed and bound by: B.O.S.S Druck und Medien GmbH
ISBN: 978-1-84126-200-0
E-Mail: info@m-m-sports.com
www.m-m-sports.com

CONTENTS

THE EXERCISES

THE PROGRAMS

CHAPTER 1

PLYOMETRICS: POWER OF PERFORMANCE

Power, the combination of speed and strength, is crucial for success in many sporting events. It is power that will dictate how hard your shots, punches or blocks are, and it will determine how quickly you respond and react to an opponent.

Power is defined as the rate at which work is performed

$$P = W \div T$$

where P is power, W is work, and T is time.

Work is defined as the application of force over some distance

$$W = F \times D$$

where F is force and D is distance.

Therefore, power is really the rate at which you can move an object, with as much force as possible.

We use the formula of $P = F \times V$, where V is velocity and comes from $D \div T$ of the $(F \times D) \div T$ power equation, as this represents a great way for athletes to understand the components of power. Therefore, in order to create large amounts of power, both the force applied and the speed at which it is applied, needs to be large. Neither great force nor speed alone can achieve great power. With this in mind, both the coach and athlete need to think explosively and always execute drills with maximal effort and speed.

Power, to be achieved, needs an optimal level of both force and velocity. This relationship is well documented in the force vs. velocity curve. It is seen below how a large force has a low velocity and consequently a low power, and that a high velocity has a low force, and thus, a low power. At point A, maximum power is attained, showing that a combination of moderate force and moderate velocity yield the highest power (Fig. 1).

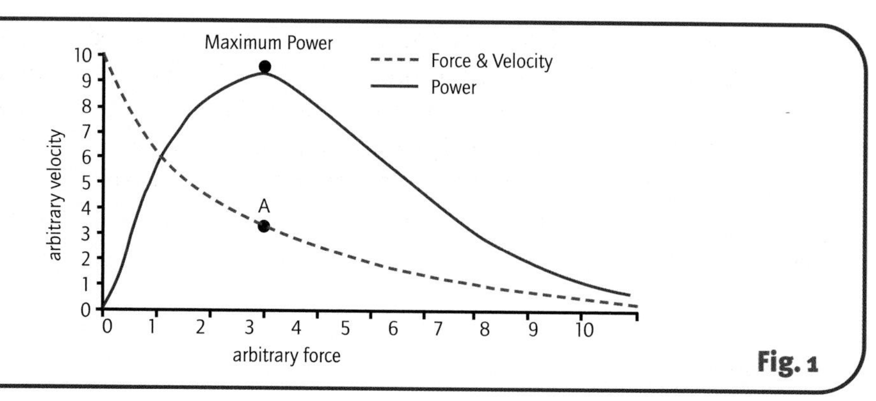

Fig. 1

In practical terms, the force velocity curve sets the limits for the speed of the execution of a movement during training. Maximum power for any activity can only be developed when the concentric phase, or the lifting phase, of the movement is performed as fast as possible.

The purpose of plyometric work is the same as that of strength training, to develop greater physical power. Many athletes spend all their time in the weight room trying to increase power with barbell and dumbbell exercises. While these exercises have their place, they are not the most efficient means of developing power. Traditional weight room exercises do not allow the athlete to move at the speed, or use the movements, needed to develop sport-specific power.

Most traditional weight room exercises follow the same pattern of force and acceleration (Figure 2). There is an initial period of acceleration followed by a deceleration as the weight approaches the sticking point of the movement, a second acceleration as the weight passes through the sticking point and a final deceleration as the weight is voluntarily stopped at the end of the range of motion.

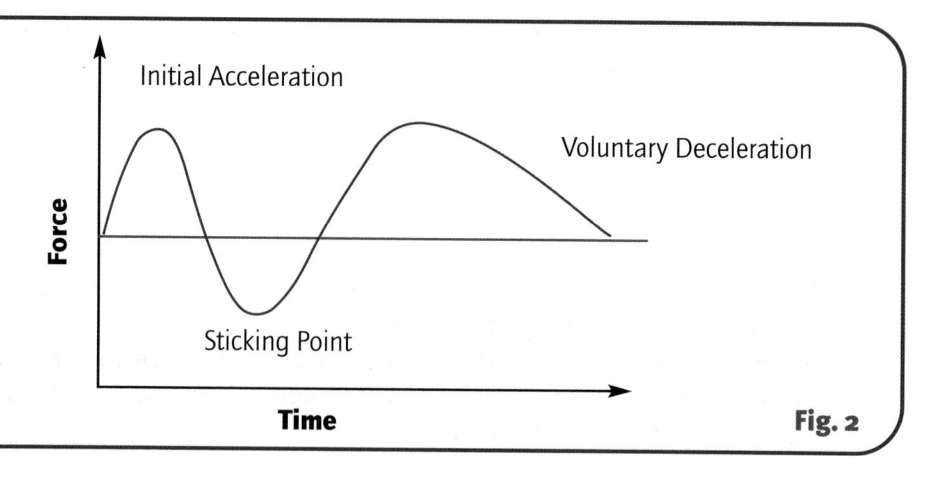

Fig. 2

The voluntary deceleration at the end of the movement is needed to stop the weight and safely perform the exercise. However, the need to slow the weight means that traditional weight training exercises cannot be performed at maximum velocity and power throughout the movement. Plyometrics, because they consist of throws and jumps, do not require a deceleration at the end of the movement, making them a more effective tool for developing maximum power through an athletic range of motion.

Plyometrics

Plyometrics are best described by understanding the mechanism of action. Plyometrics cause a muscle to rapidly stretch prior to contraction to perform a movement. That is, if a muscle undergoes a pre-stretch, it has an ability to contract more rapidly than if it just contracts on its own. This pre-stretch takes the form of a counter movement. To illustrate this concept, take a rubber band and put it on the first finger of your right hand. Now with your thumb and finger of your left hand, pull it back to take out the slack but do not stretch it. Let it go. It probably did not go very far. Do it again, but this time stretch it as far as it can and release.

The band flew across the room because of the stored elastic energy built up during the stretch. Muscles exhibit a similar action to aid the performance of powerful movments. All muscles will contract as a response to stretching. However, if trained properly, they can create an explosive force from prior stretching. Plyometrics are designed to help the muscle produce a greater force by rapidly causing it to produce that force. Most sports actions use some kind of pre-stretch prior to movement. In fact, pre-stretch may even be innate. For example, have a friend stand still and tell him/her to move rapidly sideways in the direction you point. Watch closely. Almost inevitably, the first move is to the opposite side, then in the direction you point. It appears that a pre-stretch helps propel the person to the side faster. It is no coincidence that this occurs.

Plyometric Mechanism

Stretching a muscle prior to a powerful movement is a natural reaction. This combination of eccentric-concentric contractions is known as the stretch shortening cycle and is the result of the integrated functioning of two muscle sensors; one within the tendon of the muscle called the golgi tendon organ (GTO) and the other within the muscle belly called the muscle spindle.

Muscle Spindle

The muscle spindle lies deep within the muscle itself along the fiber. It registers and sends information to the spinal cord about the stretch and length of a muscle. When it detects a severe or rapid stretch, it sends a message that returns telling the muscle to contract. While it is telling the muscle to contract, it undergoes a process known as reciprocal inhibition, which tells the opposite, antagonist, muscle not to resist the agonist muscle's contraction process. This is best illustrated by the knee cap tap test that doctors perform. When the patella tendon is tapped, it causes the quadriceps muscle to rapidly stretch, which activates the muscle spindles causing the quadriceps to contract, making the lower leg rise rapidly, while the hamstrings release from contracting, causing reciprocal inhibition.

GTO

The golgi tendon organ is responsible for registering tension and stretch changes within the tendon. This sensory mechanism is defensive in nature by acting to protect the muscle from literally tearing off the bone. When tension becomes too great, the GTO sends a signal that tells the muscle to stop contracting and causes the antagonist muscle to contract. This effect stops the movement or, at the very least, slows it down. This action is unlike the muscle spindle, which tells the same muscle to contract. It is thought that if one could reduce the action of the GTO, then its effect on the contracting muscle would be less. This would allow greater tension to develop and possibly cause strength gains. In fact, advocates practice "reducing the GTO effect" in strength training, as well as stretching and flexibility training.

Elastic Energy

When a muscle undergoes a pre-stretch, it begins to build up energy. If released promptly, as in the rubber band stretch, this energy will be able to aid in the contraction of the muscle. However, if the muscle is stretched and held too long, it will not produce an explosive effect, and in fact will make the muscle work even harder to do the same work. To illustrate this concept, try the following exercise with a partner. On a bench press, do a single complete repetition with a moderate to heavy weight starting with the arms fully extended and lowering the bar to the chest before pressing it back to the start. For your next rep, start with the bar on your chest but do not lower it yourself. Instead, start with your hands receiving the bar at your chest and have your partner hand you the bar so it is across your chest. Give it a push.

You will find this rep with the identical weight considerably harder. This also explains why the first rep in a dumbbell press is always the hardest. When using dumbbells we tend to start with the concentric portion of the lift first. Almost all barbell exercises start with the eccentric first, while machine exercises usually start with the concentric first. During the eccentric movement, the nervous system has time to tell the brain how much weight is actually there, how much stretching is occurring, and how much counter force is required for the concentric movement. With this, the GTOs and muscle spindles do their respective jobs. In a purely concentric movement, there is no elastic energy build-up, nor is there a chance for the stretch receptors to undergo a stretch. In this case, without the eccentric contraction, your muscles had no chance to gain a pre-stretch, and hence have no elastic advantage.

While not thoroughly proven, it may be noted here, that plyometric type movements can increase strength by "working on" the inhibitory nature of the GTO and muscle spindle. Through proper training, it may be possible to decrease the GTO effects while increasing the muscle spindle's ability to help execute rapid movements.

Amount of Stretch

We know a muscle will respond to stretching as a defense mechanism, but there are limits to the amount of stretching that will augment movement speed. As long as the muscle does not stretch too far past its normal range of motion, the stretch will contribute to more powerful movements. However, even though a muscle may not tear, it may be stretched too far to gain any elastic advantage or simply have the strength to perform the movement. To illustrate this idea, stand in an upright position. Slowly move your legs apart as if you were doing a "split."

At some point, you will not be able to go any farther without pulling yourself apart. And once your feet are too far apart, you cannot get up simply by contracting your adductors to stand, even if the floor surface is frictionless. Most likely you will require help to get out of the stretched position. This is similar to when you pre-stretch too far. It is not that you won't make the movement, but rather will not be able to generate superior force output.

Plyometric Sequence

Plyometric exercises always follow the same specific sequence:

- A landing phase
- An amortization phase
- Takeoff

The landing phase starts as soon as the muscles start to experience an eccentric contraction. The rapid eccentric contraction serves to stretch the elastic component of the muscle and activate the stretch reflex. A high level of eccentric strength is needed during the landing phase. Inadequate strength will result in a slow rate of stretching and poor activation of the stretch reflex.

The amortization phase, the time on the ground, is the most important part of a plyometric exercise. It represents the turn-around time from landing to takeoff and is crucial for power development. If the amortization phase is too long, the stretch reflex is lost and there is no plyometric effect.

The takeoff is the concentric contraction that follows the landing. During this phase, the stored elastic energy is used to increase jump height.

Types of Plyometrics

Plyometrics are typically divided into two categories. Single response drill and multiple response drills. Within each category, there are varying levels of intensity.

Single Response Drills

Single response jumps involve one explosive effort. Because the emphasis is on maximal effort and power in each repetition, there is a rest period between each repetition. After landing, pause to reset the starting position and focus for the next effort. Single response drills are normally done in short sets to avoid fatigue and maintain speed and power.

Jumping in place are the simplest form of plyometrics. It requires little equipment and is used for beginners to help develop jumping skills before jumps onto or over obstacles are attempted. Jumping in place can be done with either one or two legs.

Standing jumps are utilized to stress maximal effort in both the vertical and horizontal directions. These exercises are maximal efforts (one repetition), but may be repeated several times. Standing jumps are most often done onto or over boxes, hurdles, or other obstacles. Box jumps are performed by jumping for height on or over boxes (benches) from a single- or double-leg takeoff. Box jumps are fundamental plyometrics exercises that should be included in every plyo program. Hurdle jumps are performed by jumping for height over hurdles from a single- or double-leg takeoff.

Depth/drop jumps are performed by falling or jumping down from a height, followed by an immediate vertical rebound jump. Box height is one of the major considerations in the development of a depth jump program. If the boxes are too low, there will not be an overload effect on the muscle and jump improvements will be minimal. On the other hand, if the boxes are too high the athlete will have to absorb so much impact that he will lose all rebound effect from the landing. This makes the selection of an optimal box height crucial. Box height can be determined from a simple test.

The athlete first performs a maximum vertical jump. After a short rest, the athlete performs another jump from a 12-inch box and tries to reach the same height as the vertical jump test. The athlete continues to jump from progressively higher boxes (6-inch increments) until he can no longer reach the original test height. The highest height that he can jump from and still reach his test height is the maximum height box he should jump from. If the athlete is not capable of attaining his test jump height from a 12-inch box, he doesn't have enough strength to do depth jumps and should focus on strength training and lower intensity plyometrics.

Single response throws can be done from standing, sitting, or lying positions. They involve the single throw of a medicine ball or weighted object for maximum height or distance. Throws are often combined with jumps.

Multiple Response Drills

Multiple response jumps utilize the skills developed by jumping in place and in standing jumps. The exercise includes single- or double-leg jumps for distance, over multiple hurdles or onto progressively higher boxes. Multiple response jumps often include a change of direction or body orientation.

Bounds are multiple jumps for maximum distance. Bounds can be done by alternating legs in an exaggerated sprinting stride or with both legs simultaneously.

Hops are normally done over multiple objects, such as cones, or over and back across an object. The objective of hops is to jump as many times as possible in a given period of time. Hops involve jumping and landing on the same leg or both legs simultaneously. Hops are a relatively low intensity plyometric activity that can be used by beginners as well as advanced athletes.

Multiple throws involve throwing a ball back and forth to a partner. The objective is to catch and release the ball. The goal is to complete a certain number of throws in as short a time as possible or complete as many throws as possible in a given period of time.

Plyometrics are the most effective way of developing athletic power. They are a high intensity form of exercise that should be used after developing a good base of strength, body control, balance and technique.

POWER
SYSTEMS
POWER
SYSTEMS

CHAPTER 2

GETTING STARTED

Plyometrics are a very high intensity form of training, placing substantial stress on the bones, joints, and connective tissue. While plyometrics can enhance an athlete's speed, power and performance, it also places them at a greater risk of injury than less intense training methods. Prior to starting a program, there are several variables to consider so the training sessions are performed in a safe and effective manner.

Landing Surface

Plyometrics can be performed indoors or outdoors. The landing surface should be able to absorb some of the shock of landing. Gymnastic or wrestling mats are good indoor surfaces, as are the sprung wood floors found in many aerobics studios. Thick exercise mats will absorb too much impact, are unstable, and eliminate the stretch reflex needed for plyometrics. Exercise mats should be less than 15cm thick. Outdoors, plyometrics are done on the grass or sand. Jumping on concrete or asphalt can lead to knee, ankle and hip problems and should be avoided.

Equipment

One of the advantages of plyometric training is that it can be done almost anywhere with very little equipment. Most of the equipment that is needed can be made or bought at very little cost.

Cones

Plastic cones can be ordered from sporting goods catalogues and many sports stores. Several height cones are needed. Cone heights should range from 15-60cm.

Steps or Stadium Stairs

Steps are a useful plyometrics tool as long as they are safe and of suitable material. Concrete steps should be avoided because the landing surface is too hard. The stairs should be deep enough to allow the athlete to easily place his whole foot on the step. The steps should be closed to prevent the toes from getting caught under a step.

Boxes

Boxes can be constructed out of wood. A sturdy frame is covered with plywood. Several different box heights are recommended 15cm, 30cm, 45cm, and 60cm are the most common heights. Boxes of 90-145cm may be needed for advanced athletes. Angled boxes can be created for lateral jumps and drills. Boxes should be of solid construction with a non-slip surface.

Medicine Balls

Medicine balls can be made of rubber, plastic, or leather. Leather balls should only be used indoors with a partner because they are less durable than rubber or plastic balls. Medicine balls typically range in weight from 0.5-15kg. Several different weights toward the lower to middle end of this range are sufficient for most programs.

Medicine balls can be quite expensive. Individuals or institutions that are short on money can make medicine balls from old soccer balls, basketballs, or volleyballs. Cut a small hole in the ball, insert a funnel and fill the ball with sand to a desired weight. Patch the hole using a bicycle tire patch and some duct tape.

There are a variety of specialty medicine balls available. Some are the size of a baseball or softball to allow simulated throws for those sports, others are handled medicine balls, which allow single arm throws to be performed, and there are rope balls to simulate chopping and rotational movements more effectively.

Hurdles

Hurdles should be adjustable and can be made of wood or pvc piping. Hurdles can also be made by placing a dowl or taping string between two cones. Hurdle heights can vary from 30-120cm. The cross bar on the hurdle should readily fall when hit during a jump or hop.

Shoes

Footware should provide a good grip, lateral support, ankle support and still allow the foot to move naturally. Cross trainers and court shoes are better than running shoes, which often lack adequate lateral support. If landings are done on a proper surface the cushioning provided by the shoe is not very important.

Other Equipment

Shot puts, dumbbells, kettlebells, and bars can all be used for throwing and increasing resistance while jumping. Weighted vests, with adjustable weights, are a good way to increase resistance without excessive low back strain.

Physical Requirements

Medical Clearance

Athletes should have an annual physical in which joint stability and strength are assessed. Particular attention should be paid to assessing the knees and hips, particularly in female athletes, who are at greater risk of ACL injury during landings and rapid changes of direction. Any athlete with a history of spinal, shoulder, or lower limb injuries should be cautious when starting a plyometric program.

Strength or flexibility imbalances between the right and left side or between agonist and antagonist muscle groups increase the likelihood of injury during plyometrics. Strength differences between the right and left side of the body of as little as 5% can increase the risk of injury by 25 times. When returning from an injury, the athlete should have full strength in the injured area prior to returning to a plyometrics program.

Age

Plyometric training should not be done until an individual has reached puberty. The average age of onset of puberty in boys is 11 years and girls 9.5 years, lasting about two years for both genders.

Children naturally run and jump as part of play. Children know how much jumping they can do and from what height better than an adult does. Prior to puberty, children should be given the opportunity to play games that involve jumping and throwing but they should be given the option of choosing their own jump distance or height. The following guidelines should be followed when children start formal plyometrics programs:

- Young athletes require a medical examination prior to plyometric training, including assessing their physical maturity level.
- Provide adequate supervision and instruction. The athlete-coach ratio should not exceed 10:1 with a ratio of 5:1 preferred. This should help the athlete learn proper technique. Most training injuries occur because of poor exercise technique.
- Prohibit depth jumps. Depth jumps are the most intense form of plyometrics. Not allowing depth jumping helps prevent possible injury to the bones' growth zones.

- Ensure that the athlete is emotionally mature to accept and follow directions. Athletes risk injuring themselves and others when training if they cannot follow directions and safety guidelines.
- Consider the unique physical and psychological make-up of each athlete. Since the rate of emotional and physical maturity varies from person to person, an individualized training program will help improve performance and decrease the chance of injury.
- Include strength training in a conditioning program. Expose young athletes to a variety of activities and movement patterns. Limiting training to a specific activity can slow the athlete's overall development.
- Keep training fun for the athlete. By keeping training fun, the athlete can develop a lifelong appreciation of fitness and sport. The length of the athlete's career can be increased if the level of enjoyment is high.

Body Size

Large athletes, over 100kg, need to be cautious when doing plyometrics. Large athletes are at a greater risk of developing injury due to the compressive forces on the joints experienced during landing. High volume and high intensity plyometrics should be avoided. Depth jumping from a height greater than 45cm should be avoided completely.

Technical Requirements

As a general rule, an athlete should not be jumping if he does not know how to land. The next chapter includes a movement screen test that has a landing assessment component. A good landing involves the knees remaining aligned over the toes, the trunk inclined forward slightly, head up and back flat. If an athlete has difficulty maintaining this position, he should follow the Level 1 program in Chapter 10 until he has better body control and has learned the proper landing technique.

Dynamic Power Warm-Up

Warm-up is now generally regarded as an essential part of a training program. Some people perform an elaborate warm-up that often lasts almost as long as the training session. Others prefer to do a couple of stretches and then get right into training.

Ideally, a warm-up should prepare you to do the upcoming workout effectively and efficiently without creating undue fatigue. The dynamic power warm-up has been specifically designed to be used prior to plyometric training sessions and can be done in 15-20 minutes.

Goals of the Power Warm-up

Warm-up has four purposes. First, warm-up improves blood flow to the heart muscle and helps prevent abnormal cardiac rhythms and heart attack. While this may not be a major concern for younger athletes, masters athletes and athletes with very high body weight can decrease their risk of cardiac abnormalities with a good warm-up. Secondly, like the name implies, warm-up increases muscle temperature.

Increased muscle temperature results in improved oxygen uptake, decreased lactic acid production, increased speed of muscle contraction, increased force of muscle contraction, increased rate of nervous system activity, and increased range of movement. It is through these changes that performance is improved. Third, warm-up provides the ideal time for pre-competition or pre-training psychological preparation. It is the opportunity to review in your mind what is to come in the training session and develop the appropriate, aggressive mindset needed for power training. Finally, the dynamic power warm-up provides the opportunity to rehearse some of the movements to be used during training, allowing your body to perform the drills more efficiently and at a higher speed.

The prevention of injuries, such as muscle strains and tears, is often suggested as one of the primary benefits of warm-up. Even though many experts suggest that warming up can help prevent injuries, they are quick to point out that most of the evidence is empirical and that very few, if any, studies can show that warming up decreases the incidence of musculoskeletal injuries. Most muscle injuries are the result of strength or flexibility imbalances and will not be affected by warming up.

Types of Warm-ups

There are three types of warm-ups: passive, general and specific. Each has its advantages and disadvantages.

Passive Warm-up

A passive warm-up increases temperature through external means. Massage, hot showers, lotions, and heating pads are common forms. Although these methods increase body temperature, they produce little positive effect on performance. Several researchers have compared the effects of active, passive and no warm-up on physiological markers of performance. They found that the passive warm-up did not increase VO_2, or decrease blood lactate levels any more than no warm-up. They did find though that the heart rate increased. A passive warm-up, because of increased muscle temperature, may be suitable prior to a stretching exercise but should not be recommended as the sole means of warming up for intense physical activity.

General Warm-up

A general warm-up increases temperature by using movements for the major muscle groups. Calisthenics and light jogging activities are most common. This type of warm-up is meant to increase temperature in a variety of muscles using general movement patterns. This is a good warm-up for a fitness class but should not serve as the sole form of warm-up for athletic training.

Specific Warm-up

The specific warm-up is designed to prepare the participant for the specific demands of the upcoming activity. The specific warm-up helps psychological readiness, co-ordination of specific movement patterns, and prepares the central nervous system. A specific warm-up usually consists of a simulation of some technical component of the activity at work rates that increase progressively. For example, an Olympic weightlifter will perform the snatch with heavier weights progressively until reaching 80-90% of the opening attempt. Because of the rehearsal component of this type of warm-up, it is the preferred method for sports activities, particularly high speed and power activities.

Designing a Warm-up

A good warm-up has both a general and specific component and may include a passive component if the athlete feels he performs better when he uses some sort of a topical analgesic, such as Tiger Balm.

General Warm-up

Full-body Calisthenics

A warm-up starts with some full-body calisthenics. Exercises like jumping jacks, rope jumping, push ups, sit ups, and lunges are full-body exercises that will increase body temperature. These exercises should be done for only 1–2 minutes at a time as the goal of the warm-up is to increase temperature not create fatigue.

Stretching

Dynamic stretching is a more effective means of warm-up stretching than static stretching, meaning that rather than holding a stretch for a period of time, you move through a full range of motion and then back to your starting position immediately without holding the stretch. This is particularly true when you are doing power training. Several studies have shown that a static stretch immediately before power training can significantly decrease subsequent power development. This is because the static stretch decreases the effectiveness of the stretch shortening cycle discussed earlier. In the warm-up below, each of the stretches is done 4-6 times in a dynamic fashion.

Duration of General Warm-up

The amount of time needed to warm up depends on the type and intensity of the activity, as well as environmental conditions. For someone engaged in a light jogging program, 10 minutes may be sufficient for a warm-up. Elite-level athletes may require 30 or 40 minutes to warm up depending on the nature of the event, with higher intensity events requiring longer warm-ups. Exercising in a warm environment requires a shorter warm-up than exercising in a cold one. In a normal environment, the onset of sweating is usually a good indicator that body temperature has increased sufficiently.

The following is a sample general warm-up that should be followed before each of the workouts in the program chapters:

- 1 minute of jumping rope or jogging in place

10 Body Squats

Quad Stretch

Hamstring Stretch

10 Lunges

8 Jumps

10 Rotational Movements

10 Push Ups

Triceps Stretch

10 Split Jumps

Specific Warm-up

The nature of the specific warm-up depends on the activity to follow. Keep in mind that warm-up is just that, warm-up and not training. Fatigue should be kept to a minimum during warm-up otherwise the training session will suffer.

Warming Up for Strength Training

When weight training, do at least two sets, one at 50% and one at 75% of the work weight, before using the working weight. Very strong people need to do more sets. Many elite powerlifters and weightlifters use six to eight warm-up sets prior to opening attempts in competition. Repetitions in warm-up sets are low, 1–4, and done at a controlled speed. Warm-up sets are done for every exercise in the program, not just the first exercise.

Warming Up for Plyometric Training

As in weight training, a warm-up for plyometric and power events or training uses warm-up sets. Prior to each drill, start with a walk-through set that allows you to rehearse the drill in your mind and remind you of the movements and changes of direction that have to be made. Following the walk-through, perform two progressively faster trials, one at about half speed and one at three-quarter speed. Be sure to focus on good technique during each of the warm-up sets, the way you perform in the warm-up will be the way you perform in the training session.

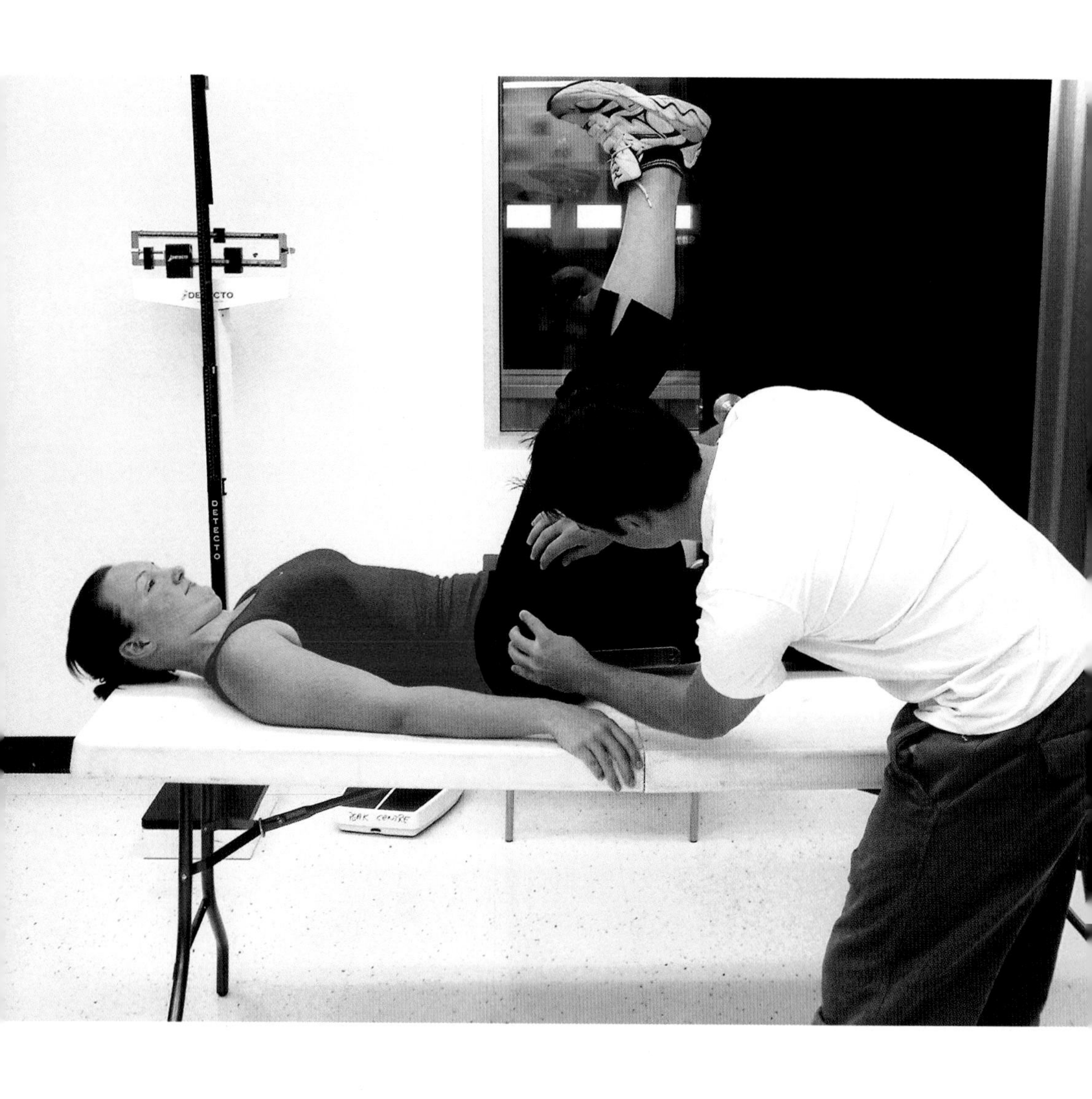
DETECTO
DETECTO

CHAPTER 3

ASSESSING YOUR STARTING POINT

Plyometrics are a high intensity form of exercise. While anyone can participate in a program of jumps, to fully benefit from a plyometric program an athlete must have adequate strength, be free of orthopedic abnormalities and have adequate strength to turn around a landing quickly, decreasing the amortization phase as much as possible. Prior to starting a plyometric program, there are several evaluations and sets of tests that should be conducted.

Movement Screening

The ability to control your body and perform basic movements is essential for every sport. Weakness and muscle imbalances can lead to chronic injuries that can cost you a season and detract from the enjoyment of the sport. Prior to starting a plyometric program, everyone should go through a basic movement screen that will help them choose their starting level and appropriate exercises to help them maximize their progress.

Step Up

The step up is a test of hip strength, particularly the glutes, and hip abductors, muscles that are extremely important for explosive jumping and landing. Subjects who are unable to pass this test have a strength deficiency that causes the knee to be unstable when jumping or landing, increasing their risk of ACL injuries during jumping or cutting activities.

The box or bench used for this exercise needs to be high enough to create a 120-degree angle at the knee when the foot is placed on the box. Stand 12-18 inches behind the box or bench. Place the entire foot of one leg on the top of the box, shifting the body weight to the leg on the box. Powerfully extend the knee, hip, and ankle of the foot on the box, and bring the body to a standing position on top of the box. Step off the box, keeping all body weight on the working leg and lightly touch the ground with the non-working leg, do not put any weight on the non-working leg, as it is only being used as a guide for depth. Immediately stand back up. Keep the trunk upright throughout the movement; avoid bending over at the waist. Perform five reps on each leg.

Scoring System

When doing this exercise, your weight is always on the foot that is on the bench. Even when in the bottom position, the back foot should not be loaded. If the subject pushes off and the back foot or the whole foot touches down, give him 2 points.

Your knee should stay aligned with your foot. If the knee tracks to the inside of the foot so that the center of the knee is inside the big toe, this is an indicator of weakness in the glutes and abductors and earns the subject 3 points.

The subject must maintain an upright body position at all times. If the subject bends at the waist, this removes the glutes from the exercise, making it more of a quadriceps exercise. If the subject bends at the waist, give him 3 points.

The points for this exercise are additive, meaning that pushing off the back leg and the knee pulling to the inside of the toe would give the subject 5 points. If there is a visible performance difference between right and left legs, the subject receives 7 points.

If no errors occur, the subject gets zero points.

Box Landing
In order to safely and effectively perform jumps and agility drills, an athlete must have proper landing mechanics – he must land on the balls of the feet, with the knees bent and aligned with the 2nd and 3rd toes, trunk upright, and head up.

The box-landing test will require a 12-18 inch (30-45cm) box and an appropriate landing area, like a sprung wood floor or a rubber-matted surface. The subject will stand upright on the box and hop off landing with both feet simultaneously. Repeat the test five times.

If the subject lands with toes aligned over the middle toes, trunk upright and on the balls of the feet without stepping forward, he receives 0 points.
If the subject lands and the knees pull inward or he must take a step to balance themselves he receives 3 points.
If the subject lands and he bends forward with their trunk he will receive 3 points.
If the subject lands and the knees move inward and the trunk comes forward, he receives 5 points.

Correct Wrong

Lateral Hop Landing
You will need masking tape or duct tape and a tape measure for this test.

Place a piece of tape on the floor. Stand on one foot with your hands behind your back, foot on the tape. Bend the leg to about 90°, swing the other leg and jump sideways as far as possible. Repeat for four jumps in each direction.

The subject should be able to land the jump with the knee of the landing foot over the middle two toes, trunk upright and head up.

The subject is given 2 points if he does not stick the landing and moves his foot or takes a second hop upon landing. He receives 3 points if the trunk comes forward during the landing and his back rounds. Five points are given if the subject's knee tracks to the big toe or inside the toes and 7 points are given for any combination of the above.

Lateral Hop Distance

Bilateral muscle imbalances, an imbalance between the right and left side of the body, have been implicated in the development of injury. A muscle imbalance of greater than 10% can increase the risk of injury by 20 times. The lateral hop test can be used to assess differences in strength and power in the power body muscles. Using the distances jumped in the previous test, plug the numbers into the formula below and calculate the percent difference in distance jumped between the right and left sides of the body. Perform four jumps with each leg.

(Right/ Left) – 1 x 100 = percent difference

Difference	Score
< 3%	0 points
3%-5%	2 points
5%-10%	3 points
10%-15%	5 points
> 15%	7 points

Single Leg Lying Hamstring Raise

The subject lies flat on his back with legs straight and hands just out from his sides. With one leg flat against the ground, the other leg is kept straight and lifted as high as possible. Using a goniometer, the raised leg angle is measured with the head of the trochanter as the axis of rotation. Perform three trials on each leg and record the best score. Scoring is as follows:

Difference	Score
>90°	0 points
75°-90°	2 points
60°-75°	3 points
45°-60°	5 points
<45°	7 points

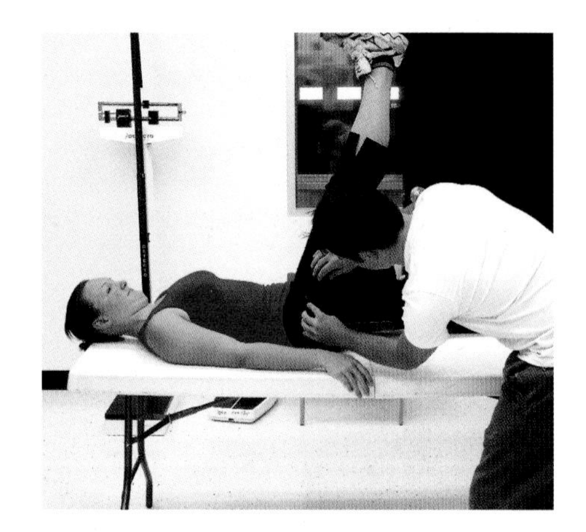

One-Legged Balance T-Test

Have the subject raise his arms to his sides so that they are parallel to the floor. Stand on one leg and rotate from the hip so that the upper body and non-support leg are parallel to the floor. There should be a straight line from the top of the head through to the toes of the non-support leg; the supporting leg is slightly bent at the knee. Shoulders are squared to the floor, not rotated. This position must be held for 10 seconds to fully pass the test. Repeat on the other leg.

If the subject cannot hold the position for the full 10 seconds, he is given 1 point. If the subject cannot get his back leg or trunk parallel, he receives 2 points. If neither reaches parallel, 3 points are awarded. This test is a measure of balance and stability not kinesthetic sense, so the tester can provide verbal feedback and correction to a subject who is having difficulty getting his body in the right position but cannot actively move the subject into the appropriate position. The time starts when proper position is achieved.

If there is a difference between the right and left sides of the body, the subject is given 5 points.

Push Up Hold

This test measures upper body and trunk strength. The subject starts lying face down with hands by the shoulders in a push up position; the thumbs are just under the shoulders. Keeping the body straight so that only the toes are on the ground, push half-way up until there is a 90-degree angle at the elbows. When the subject gets into position, the timer is started and this position is held as long as possible. The body must be kept straight during the whole movement; the test is stopped when the subject cannot hold a straight body or 90 degrees at the elbows. Scoring is as follows:

Difference	Score
0-10s	7 points
10-20s	5 points
20-30s	3 points
30-40s	2 points
40s+	0 points

Prone Pull Up

This test measures strength of the back and arm muscles. Set a bar in a power cage so that when the subject is lying on his back directly below the bar, it is 6-8cm beyond his reach. Tie a piece of string or dynaband around the power cage uprights 15cm below the bar.

The subject reaches up and grasps the bar with an overhand grip. The hands are positioned so that there is 60cm between the index fingers. The body is straight throughout the movement with only the heels touching the floor. A pull up is counted when the subject's chin passes the string or elastic band. The subject performs as many pull ups as possible. If he cannot hold the proper body position for two consecutive pull ups or three out of every four the test is stopped. Score as follows:

Difference	Score
0-10	5 points
11-15	3 points
16-20	2 points
21-25	1 point
26+	0 points

Lying Leg Raise

The lying leg raise is a test of rectus abdominus and external oblique strength. As the legs are lowered toward the floor, the force developed by the hip flexors tends to tilt the pelvis anteriorly, creating resistance against the rectus abdominus and external obliques, which are holding the pelvis in posterior tilt.

The subject lies flat on his back with legs straight and hands across his chest. Help the subject raise his legs until they are perpendicular to the ground. Holding the pelvis in a posterior tilt, contract the trunk muscles and pull the lower back tight against the floor.

Keeping the legs straight and lower back against the floor, slowly lower the legs toward the floor. When the lower back first lifts off the floor, the angle between the legs and table is measured with a goniometer using the head of the trochanter as the axis of rotation. The following scoring system is used:

Difference	Score
< 15°	0 points
15°- 45°	2 points
45°-60°	3 points
60°-90°	5 points
Cannot keep back flat	7 points

Excessively tight hamstrings may prevent the subject from achieving a proper starting position. A poor score on the lying hamstring raise will indicate if this is the case. If the subject cannot lower his legs slowly, this may be caused by very weak hip flexors. To determine this, have the subject lie in the starting position and try to raise his legs off the floor. If the legs cannot be lifted, the hip flexors are too weak to perform the test and need to become a training priority.

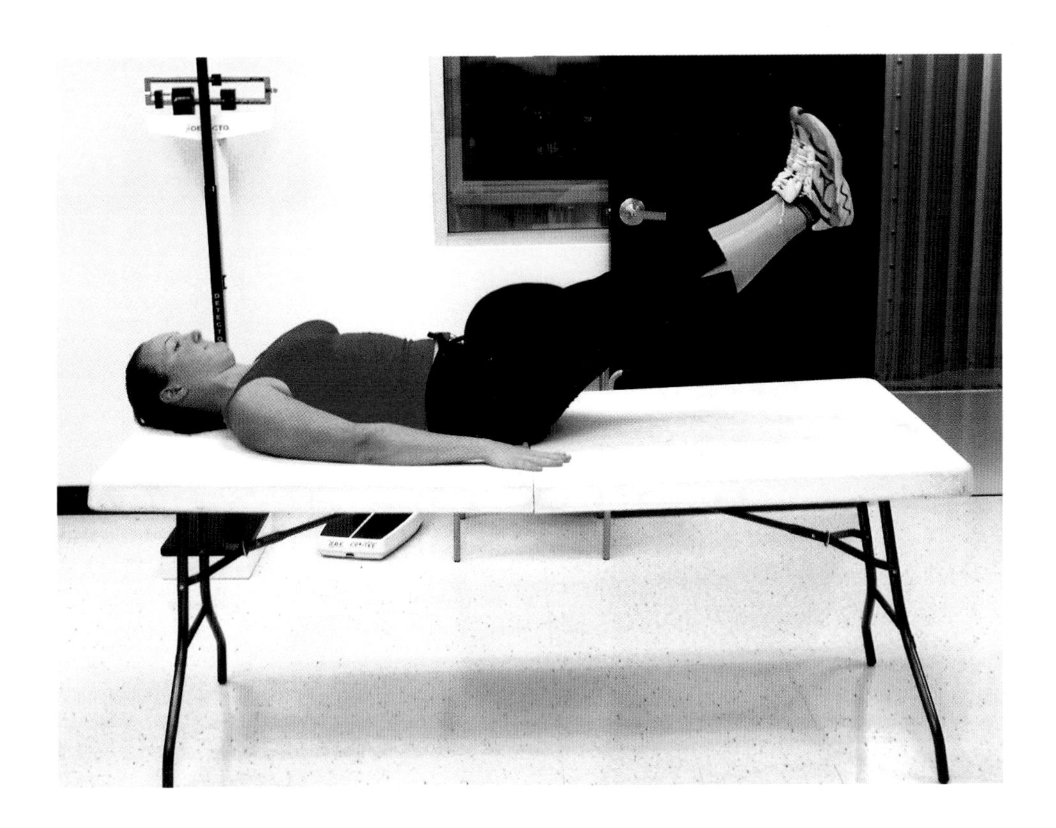

Interpreting the Data

Once all tests have been completed, total the subject's score. Three ranges of scores are used to determine the type and level of program that is most appropriate for the client.

Level 1

Score: 40+

Those athletes who fall in this group exhibit marked weakness throughout their body that contributes to poor movement control and execution. They are not capable of working against their body weight while keeping their body properly aligned. These athletes are at the greatest risk for developing injuries during high speed and power activities. A traditional program of plyomteric drills is far too advanced for these athletes. Training programs should focus on basic movement and body control drills.

- Ground-based balance activities, both single and double legged.
- Emphasizing the mastery of basic body positions and movements like squatting, running forwards and backwards, shuffling, crawling and climbing.
- Abdominal strengthening
- Lightweight medicine balls and other light implements, like rubber tubing, should be used in place of push ups and other body weight exercises.
- The mechanics of body position change should be emphasized during low speed turns, cuts and corners.
- Landing mechanics from low level boxes or steps.
- Obstacle courses built around climbing over, crawling under and stepping over or around various objects.
- Adolescent and post-adolescent subjects should begin a weight training program that emphasizes hip and trunk strength using large multi-joint exercises.
- Flexibility training.

Movements to avoid include:

- Rapid changes of direction
- Single leg jumps
- Multiple response jumps
- Olympic-style lifts
- Jumps off boxes or objects more than 12 inches high
- Single limb isolation strength exercises
- Equipment-based balance training

Level 2

Score: 22-39

Clients scoring in this range have moderate weakness or strength imbalances that affect their body control and predispose them to injury during high speed and power activities. They still require a significant amount of work on basic movement skills but are capable of handling higher intensity drills and exercises. A strength program featuring large multi-joint movements should be the emphasis of a balanced program that includes:

- Ground-based and equipment-based balance drills
- Free weight and body weight exercises
- Basics change of direction drills
- Low-level two-legged jumps and hops over hurdles
- Two-legged ladder drills
- Single response jumps onto boxes with landing
- Flexibility
- Abdominal strengthening
- Rotational drills

Movements to avoid include:

- Multiple response jumps
- Single leg jumps and hops
- Depth jumping
- Olympic-style lifts

Level 3
Score: 0-21

Those clients who fall into level three have good body control and no major strength deficits that increase their risk of injury. These clients are able to perform most types of training safely and effectively as long as proper exercise progressions are followed. Technical errors in cutting, running, jumping, cornering and landing are most likely due to true technique and learning errors and not strength or flexibility imbalances. Time still needs to be spent on reinforcing basic movement skills, but there are not restrictions on the type of exercises performed as long as the following progression is respected:

Drill Type	Intensity	Example
Hops	Low	Rope hops, Calf hops, Octagon hops, Pattern hops, Lunges
Cuts, Corners and Turns	Low	90° cut, 180° turn, M drill, T-drill, Up and Back, Reaction drills.
Two-Foot Ladder drills	Low	Icky shuffle, chain saws, Ladder runs forward backward and lateral; Two-legged ladder hops forward, backward and lateral
Double Limb Single Response jump and throws	Low-Moderate	Vertical jump, Standing long jump, Box jump, Pike Jump, Tuck jump, Overhead toss, Med. ball chest pass
Full-body Single Response throws	Moderate	Med. ball vertical jump and toss, Med. ball backwards toss, Med. ball long jump and toss, Shot put, Rotational throws
Double-Limb Multiple Response jumps and throws	Moderate-High	Multiple long jumps, Repeat vertical jumps, Box jump and leap, Speed box jumps, Rope jumps
Single-Limb Single Response Jumps and Throws	High	Single-leg vertical jump, Single leg long jump, One-arm chest pass
Single-limb ladder drills	High	Single-leg slaloms, Single-leg hops (forward, backward and lateral)
Single-Limb Multiple Response Jumps and Throws	Very High	Repeat Single-leg long jumps, Single-leg pattern hops

Performance Testing

If an athlete scores level 3 in the movement screening, he can move onto performance testing to help determine if further strengthening is needed to allow him to get the most out of his plyometric program.

Jump tests

Jump tests are general tests of power that are simple to perform, require little equipment and are safe for almost everyone. Jump testing involves both static jumps, without a preload, and countermovement jumps, where the athlete is allowed to dip or preload prior to jumping.

Static Vertical Jump (SVJ)

The static vertical jump measures concentric lower body power. To perform the static jump, you will need gym chalk, a tape measure and a high wall. Chalk the middle finger of one hand, standing perpendicular to the wall so that the chalked hand is close to the wall. Reach as high as possible and place a mark on the wall. Step 6-8 inches from the wall and squat down as far as you can while keeping your feet flat on the floor. Without dipping downward, jump as high as you can, swinging the arms, reaching as high as possible to place a second mark on the wall. Repeat for 3-5 trials. Measure the distance between reaching height and maximum jump height to the nearest inch.

Counter Movement Vertical Jump (CMJ)

The countermovement vertical jump, when compared to the static vertical jump, assesses the contribution of the stretch shortening cycle to power performance. The set up for the countermovement jump is similar to that of the static jump. The countermovement jump starts from a standing position. Then rapidly dip down and jump as high as possible, swinging the arms and reaching as high as possible to place a mark on the wall. Repeat for 3-5 trials, then measure the distance between the reaching height and the maximum jump height.

Running Vertical Jump (RVJ)

The running vertical jump assesses the stretch shortening cycle under a higher load. A Vertec or other jump measurement device is needed to perform the running vertical jump. Starting 3-5 steps from the device, run up to the Vertec and perform a two-leg jump, swinging the arms and reaching as high as possible. Repeat for 3-5 trials, recording the best jump. Subtract this score from the reaching height to calculate vertical jump height.

Interpreting the Data

The countermovement vertical jump is the jump most people are familiar with and the one that they are referring to when discussing how high they can jump.

The static vertical jump can be combined with the countermovement jump to determine the effectiveness of the stretch shortening cycle. The countermovement vertical jump should be at least 15% greater than your static vertical jump.

If your difference is less than 15%, you should perform a 1RM squat test, to determine if strength is adequate. If you score above 1.2 times body weight on the squat test, you are getting most of your jump power from strength and may benefit from learning to use the stretch shortening cycle more effectively by incorporating plyometrics into your program. If you score below 1.2 times body weight on the squat test, strength is a problem and needs to be developed before proceeding into a plyomeric program.

A difference of greater than 15% between CMJ and SVJ indicates that you are using the stretch shortening cycle efficiently and need to increase strength to see further gains in jump height and power.

The running vertical jump can be used to further test your ability to use the stretch shortening cycle. The RVJ should be higher than both your SVJ and CMJ. The RVJ tests your ability to quickly change your momentum and develop power in the opposite direction. If the RVJ is less than your CMJ, your ability to change direction under load needs work by increasing the eccentric strength in the lower body.

Jump testing, when the arms are used, measures full body power. A well-timed and explosive arm swing can account for 15-20% of jump height. In order to isolate the lower body, the same jumps described above can be used but the hands are held above the head throughout the jump. Removing the arm swing will result in jump heights that are about 15% lower than with the arms. If you do not see this sort of difference, shoulder power may be limiting your jump performance.

1RM Tests

1RM testing measures the ability to lift a maximum weight in selected exercises. The 1RM testing allows you to compare your current strength level to the goal levels and adjust priorities in your training program, increasing or decreasing the emphasis on strength training depending on whether or not you have reached the strength goals.

The procedure used for the 1RM testing is as follows:

- Warm up with a light weight that can easily be handled for 5-10 reps
- Rest 2 minutes
- Increase the weight by 10-20% and do a second warm-up of 3-5 reps
- Rest 2 minutes
- Increase the weight by another 10-20% and perform a final warm-up of 2-3 reps
- Rest 3-4 minutes
- Increase the load by 5-10% and try one repetition
- Rest 3-4 minutes
- If the last attempt was successful, increase the weight by 3-5% and try another repetition. If it was not successful, decrease the weight by 2.5-5% and try again.
- Repeat this process until only one repetition can be performed with proper technique. Always rest 3-4 minutes between attempts.

Ideally, the 1RM will be found within five sets of finishing the warm-up. If it takes longer than this, fatigue may affect the accuracy of the test. The exercises chosen for testing, squat, bench press, and deadlift have been chosen because they form the core of most strength programs and cover all the major muscle groups used in most plyometric exercises.

Squat

The high bar squat technique is typically used to allow trunk angles to be more similar to those experienced in jumping. Stand with feet slightly wider than shoulder width apart. Place the bar across the trapezoids midway between the top of the posterior deltoid and C7, resting on the trapezoids. Hands should be placed just outside the shoulders with the elbows pointing straight down. Feet point outward at about 30° angles. Keeping the head up and looking straight ahead helps the athlete stabilize his trunk. Squat depth achieves a knee angle just below parallel as this allows the large muscles of the hips to be involved in the exercise.

Bench Press

Lie on your back on a bench press bench with feet spread wide, flat on the floor. Reach up and grasp the bar with an overhand grip, placing your hands just wider than shoulder width apart. Inhale deeply and lift the bar out of the rack to arm's length. Lower the bar under control so that it touches your chest near the base of your sternum; do not bounce the bar off your chest. Press the bar back up to arm's length. Keep your feet planted firmly and your head, shoulders and buttocks in contact with the bench throughout the movement.

Deadlift

Stand with feet about hip width apart, shins close to the bar, feet pointing straight ahead. Squat down and grasp the bar with an overhand grip. The starting position should be similar to that of a power clean from the floor. Make sure the athlete keeps his hips down at the start of the movement and initiates the movement with his legs. The athlete must come to a full, straight standing position with shoulders back for the lift to count.

Interpreting the Data

Strength can be classified as absolute or relative. Absolute strength refers to the maximum amount of weight that can be lifted regardless of body weight. For instance, a powerlifter who weighs 300lbs and bench presses 325lbs has greater absolute strength than a powerlifter who weighs 200lbs and bench presses 320lbs. Relative strength refers to the level of strength in relation to body weight. Relative strength is much more important for sports where success depends on the ability to accelerate the body. When measuring strength for plyometric activities, it is expressed as a relative strength score, a proportion of body weight. The table below provides some guidelines for adequate strength levels for various types of athletes.

Strength to Weight Goals for Men

	Racquet sports	Sprinting Sports	Jumping sports
Squat	1.1-1.4	1.4-1.6	1.6-2.0
Bench Press	1.0-1.25	1.0-1.25	1.0-1.25
Deadlift	1.1-1.4	1.4-1.6	1.8-2.0

Strength to Weight Goals for Women

	Racquet sports and throwing	Sprinting Sports	Jumping sports
Squat	0.8-1.0	1.0-1.3	1.4-1.7
Bench Press	0.5-0.7	0.5-0.7	0.5-0.7
Deadlift	0.8-1.0	1.0-1.3	1.4-1.7

There are differences in the strength levels required for the various categories of sport because the type of plyometric drills used gets progressively more difficult as you move across the table. Some sports combine both sprinting and jumping or throwing and sprinting; in these cases, use the category with the higher strength requirements.

Follow-up Testing

One of the purposes of these tests is to determine an appropriate starting level and what needs to be trained, but they can also be used to measure progress and provide a basis for adjusting and individualizing the training program.

These tests should be performed at the start of the off-season, preseason and post season to monitor your progress. Sport-specific performance and fitness tests, like the 40-yard dash in football or home to second sprint in baseball, should be conducted every 8 weeks throughout the year. While progress will not be seen or expected at every test session because of the focus of the training program; the tests will ensure that speed, strength and power are being properly maintained.

Care should be taken if testing is done during the competitive season; avoid testing in the 2-3 weeks prior to a major competition or championship game. Testing close to a major competition does not provide the athlete or coach time to adjust the program to correct any weakness or problems that are found.

Poor tests are common at this time of year in individual sports where athletes only compete in a few key competitions, fatigue is high because of the intense training and competition schedule prior to the major taper of the year. A poor test, can be psychologically devastating to a team or individual. Athletes may start to question their preparation and the coach's ability to develop a championship program, leading to a negative mindset going into the most important competition of the year.

CHAPTER 4

DESIGNING A PLYOMETRIC PROGRAM

Plyometrics are a very high intense training that can quickly lead to overtraining and overuse injuries if the training program is not carefully planned. The proper manipulation of volume, total number of repetitions, and intensity decreases the risks associated with this training method.

Determining Training Intensity

Intensity is a measure of how hard you work, often compared to the maximum amount that you can do. It is a factor in determining the overall stress a training session creates. As a power training technique, the speed of movement and power produced in each rep of plyometric training determines whether or not you will get a training adaptation. All repetitions in a plyometric exercise are performed at maximum speed and power, anything less deceases the stretch shortening response and plyometric effect of the movement.

The overall intensity of the workout is determined by the drills and exercises selected. Table 1 ranks the relative intensity of plyometrics by drill type for low to high intensity movements. While there are several hundred plyometric movements, this classification system will help you to determine what you should do, as well as help you create your own program. The intensity level is determined by the initial pre-stretch or counter movement prior to the actual movement itself.

Intensity is also determined by the degree of difficulty in performing the movement, and the landing. Lunges would be classified as low intensity because there is little countermovement or pre-stretch required, and the landing is very light. Jumping off a box, landing, then rapidly jumping again would be considered high intensity. A moderate intensity movement would be performing a vertical jump. Whether you land on one leg or two, the intensity level is still determined by the initial movement, i.e., taking off on one leg is higher intensity than taking off on two legs.

Table 1. *Relative Intensity of Various Plyometric Drills and Exercises*

Drill Type	Intensity	Example
Hops	Low	Rope hops, Calf hops, Octagon hops, Pattern hops, Lunges
Double-Limb Single Response Jumps and Throws	Low-Moderate	Vertical jump, Standing long jump, Box jump, Pike Jump, Tuck jump, Overhead toss, Med ball chest pass
Full-body Single Response Throws	Moderate	Med. ball vertical jump and toss, Med. ball backwards toss, Med. ball long jump and toss, Shot put, Rotational throws
Double-Limb Multiple Response Jumps and Throws	Moderate-High	Multiple long jumps, Repeat vertical jumps, Box jump and leap, Speed box jumps, Rope jumps
Single-Limb Single Response Jumps and Throws	High	Single-leg vertical jump, Single-leg long jump, One-arm chest pass
Single-Limb Multiple Response Jumps and Throws	Very High	Repeat Single-leg long jumps, Single-leg pattern hops

When progressing with your exercises, it is important to understand what constitutes a progressive step. In other words, since it is important to perform all movements at 100% intensity, increasing speed of performance to increase difficulty level doesn't make sense. Rather, to progress from medium to high intensity, for example, you would increase the height of the box, which in turn increases the possible pre-stretch. Or you may increase the length of a jump, or the distance and duration of an exercise. Unfortunately, there are too many exercises to discuss every single movement, but a guideline would be that generally the higher and longer the distance covered is and the faster the movement is performed, the higher the intensity level.

Establishing Intensity in Each Set

Intensity in each set is a little more difficult to monitor. Many coaches count on the athlete's perceived exertion and their understanding that plyometrics need to be maximal effort. Unfortunately, many athletes are capable of pushing themselves in a workout and feel that they are giving a maximum effort even when their body is on the verge of overtraining. A quantitative measurement of performance provides the athlete and coach with a more precise way of determining training intensity.

The 10% Drop-Off Rule

Plyometrics, like strength training, are planned using sets and reps. In a strength training workout, intensity is controlled by the amount of resistance. If 80% of 1RM is on the bar, the athlete will reach a failure point at about 10-12 reps. Unlike strength training, sets of a plyometrics exercise are never taken to the point of muscular failure, making it more difficult to determine when an athlete stops benefiting from the set. During plyometric training it is necessary to base the duration of a set on drops in power and energy.

Energy is the limiting factor in all power activities. The amount of energy you can produce determines both the amount of and duration of work. During high intensity plyometric activity, the body relies primarily on the, adenosine triphosphate and creatine phosphate (ATP-CP) stored in the muscles for energy. The ATP-CP system is the most powerful energy system in the body, producing huge amounts of energy in a very short period of time. Unfortunately, the supply of ATP-CP is limited, and the energy system is quickly depleted, resulting in a drop in speed and power. The rate of depletion of the ATP-CP system depends on the type of drill but is generally limited to 5-15 seconds of continuous all-out work. As this energy system becomes depleted, there is a gradual decrease in power output, which can be measured as a decrease in performance.

Power outputs below 90% of max are insufficient to create a speed and power training effect. Once power drops below 90% of max, the set should be terminated. Determining this power drop is a relatively easy procedure, requiring only a stopwatch, measuring tape, calculator and some good record keeping. Let's look at an example using a single response vertical jump: After a good warm-up, chalk your fingers, reach as high as possible and put a mark on the wall. Step back and jump as high as possible, putting a mark on the wall. After three jumps, take a tape measure and measure the best height jumped, using the difference between reaching height and jump height as your score. After doing a quick calculation , subtracting 10% from the best height, place another mark on the wall, representing the minimum height you need to obtain on each jump. When two consecutive reps are below the 90% line, the set is stopped. After a short rest, perform another set until you once more fail to reach the 90% line then rest again. You may not get the same number of repetitions in each set. This is fine since it represents the amount of fatigue that carries over from set to set. As long as you stay above 90% of your best, you will be getting the speed and power training effect you are looking for. Repeat this procedure for the total number of reps required.

The system outlined above uses the best score on each training day. An alternative is to use a 10% drop from the best score obtained during a scheduled test session. The advantage to this is that the calculation only has to be done once following the test session, making it quicker and easier to administer for coaches who are working with large groups of athletes. Unfortunately, relying on test results doesn't allow you to adjust the program for the improvements you make between test sessions. If you decide to use test results, schedule retests every four weeks and make sure you test each exercise and drill that is going to be in the program.

Whether you base your 10% drop on test results or the best for each training session you should do a formal test session at least every 6-8 weeks to ensure the program is delivering the desired results.

Contacts per Session

Plyos are recorded by the number of single-foot contacts with the ground. For example, 80 contacts would be 4 sets of 10 reps with a two-legged type movement or a total of 80 steps with walking lunges. The volumes listed in Table 2 represent the total number of contacts per training session, not the number of contacts per exercise. This table assumes that each movement is at 100% effort. Plyometrics performed at anything less than 100% does not get the benefit associated with rapid elastic force production. However, new plyo drills should be done at 70%-80% until you are comfortable and confident with the technique of the exercise.

Table 2

Level	Low Intensity	Medium Intensity	High Intensity
Beginner	80	60	40
Intermediate	100	80	60
Advanced	140	120	100

Plyometrics should not be performed more than twice per week unless you are training specifically for a sport that requires rapid change movement. If you are looking to incorporate them into your current conditioning program, two sessions per week is adequate.

Rest Between Sets

Rest and recovery are crucial variables in a plyo program. Rest refers to the time that is taken between each exercise or set. Recovery, discussed in the periodization chapter refers to the amount of time that is needed before the workout can be repeated.

The amount of rest that is taken depends upon the duration of work and the type of drill or exercise used, varying from 0-7 minutes between sets or exercises. Table 3 summarizes the duration of work and rest periods for a variety of work periods. In this table, the work period refers to the period of continuous work and may not represent the total time for each set. In the case of single response drill, it is common to take 5-10 seconds between reps to reset your body position. This can make the total time for the set quite long even though the continuous work time is very short, usually less than one second.

Table 3. *Work and Rest Periods*

Work Time	Rest between reps	Rest between sets	Rest between exercises
< 1s	5-10 s	1-2 minutes	None
1-3 seconds	None	2-3 minutes	None
4-15 seconds	None	2-4 minutes	None
15-30 seconds	None	3-5 minutes	5-10 minutes

Note that the rest periods between sets are not less than 2 minutes unless the work period is very short. It is important to keep rest periods of this duration rather than trying to work on the 30-60-second rest periods that are often recommended in popular magazines. Short rest periods will limit the total amount of work that can be done and thereby decrease the effectiveness of the training program.

Very short rest periods do not allow a complete recovery of the ATP-CP energy system or time for removal of lactic acid. Plyo drills, with sets of fewer than 8 repetitions, use predominantly the ATP-CP energy system. These two compounds, known as the phosphagens, are available for immediate use. The stored supply of these compounds is relatively small; they can provide energy for about 5-15 seconds of allout effort. Once all the stored energy is used, the body requires about 3 minutes to fully replace the phosphagens. If the next set is started before the phosphagens are fully restored, the muscles will be forced to use the anaerobic lactic energy system. This will result in a build up of lactic acid.

Lactic acid is responsible for the burning sensation in the muscles. It also causes feelings of heaviness and fatigue. Contrary to popular belief, lactic acid does not promote increases in muscular size, strength, or power. In fact, a build up of lactic acid will inhibit the quantity and quality of work performed resulting in fewer power gains.

Lactic acid, an acidic end product of anaerobic glycolysis, can decrease the pH level in the muscle. The enzymes that are responsible for energy production are very sensitive to changes in pH. When the pH level drops, these enzymes stop functioning and the muscle fibers can no longer produce energy. As a result of the shut down in energy production the muscle fibers are no longer capable of participating in the exercise. When enough muscle fibers drop out of the exercise, the weight cannot be lifted anymore. Training using the alactic energy system can decrease the chance of muscle fiber drop out. Lactic acid also interferes with the release and uptake of calcium in the muscle, which is necessary for muscle contraction to occur.

If enough time is not left between sets, lactic acid will accumulate not only in the muscle but in the blood, as well. Once in the blood, the lactic acid is transported to all parts of the body. When lactic acid is transported to other muscles, it negatively affects their performance also. In other words, training one muscle group to failure is going to decrease the quantity and quality of work done by another muscle group.

A build up of lactic acid can increase the chance of injury. When muscle fibers start to drop out of an exercise, technique starts to get sloppy. Muscle fiber dropout also makes it more difficult for motor patterns to be established, i.e., people who are doing a new exercise will have greater difficulty learning the exercise if they are producing high levels of lactic acid.

While shorter rest periods will make you think that you are working harder in the long run, you are only defeating the purpose of plyometric training by producing less power because of artificial fatigue.

Selecting Drills and Exercises

Some people don't want a long explanation of how to determine the best drills for their sport, they are content with being told which drills to do. This is fine for the sports with a large participation base whose programs show up in Part III of this book. They can simply look at the sample programs and with some minor modifications to suit their situation have a sport-specific program. For those who are involved in sports with smaller participation bases or who just prefer to have complete control over the development of their training program, selecting or creating the best drills and exercises is a critical component of designing their program.

There are two dominant schools of thought on how to choose exercises for a sports conditioning program. There is the generalist camp, that believes in training general physical abilities that are common to all sports. These people often say they are practicing functional training. There is also the specificity of training camp that believes in mimicking sports skills while under load. To fully understand how to incorporate plyometrics into a training program, both view points need to be considered.

Specificity of Training

Specificity of training has a broad variety of meanings and can be applied to energy systems, movement patterns, and speed of movement. In simplest terms, specificity means training for the specific demands of the sport by simulating all or parts of the performance during a training session. The concept of specificity is based on transfer of training, which refers to the amount of fitness improvement that carries over to competition. For instance, if you increased your bench press by 100% but only increased your playing ability by 2%, you would have had a 2% transfer of training. Proponents of specificity believe that the more closely you simulate a sport movement, the greater the transfer of training. There is ample evidence to support this notion both in motor learning literature and anecdotes. Think about the tennis player who takes up squash for the first time. He will be relatively successful the first time he plays squash because the movements he uses in tennis are close enough to those used in squash that there is a high level of transfer. This is not to say that the tennis player will become a top squash player, it is only meant to highlight the idea that by training movement patterns that are close to those of your sport, you can affect an improvement in your sport.

In terms of plyometrics, specificity would mean creating drills and exercises that copy all or parts of the movement patterns most used in a sport. For instance, a volleyball player would do standing vertical jumps at a net with his hands up in a blocking stance rather than using the arm swing typical of vertical jump. He may also prefer to do a two step vertical jump that simulates the approach and takeoff rather than a standing vertical jump. A baseball player may opt for throwing a heavier ball or swinging a heavier bat, in an attempt to use the same movement patterns he does in his sport.

One major disadvantage to building a program solely using specificity is that many sports skills are changed when they are attempted under heavier loading. While many people feel that swinging a heavier bat during the off-season will increase strength and bat speed, in reality the heavier bat changes the batting technique enough that there is actually very little increase in bat speed. In some extreme cases, sports skills can be changed enough that when the athlete switches back to training with normal loads, he finds his skills have changed, often for the worse as he has adopted the pattern learned under heavier load.

Many sports have very unpredictable movement patterns. A running back never knows how he is going to have to move on any given play. A wrestler never knows what position he is going to find himself in. This can make it difficult to design a specific program that addresses all the movement patterns an athlete needs, causing some important but uncommon patterns to be overlooked.

General Physical Abilities Training

Many types of training can create similar adaptations in the body's systems. For instance, both long distance running and interval training improve the cardiovascular system, enhancing aerobic fitness. Those who favor general physical abilities training base their programs on the weakness of specificity, believing that sports skills cannot properly be simulated under loaded conditions and that combining specific skill work with training of the body's physical systems will allow the physical conditioning to best transfer to performance. Again, there is both a sound scientific basis and anecdotal evidence to support this method of training.

Trainers who focus on general physical abilities will use a variety of drills and exercises to address common movements seen in a variety of sports. They would include vertical, horizontal, and lateral jumps in a plyo program, as well as a variety of full-body drills, combining jumps and throws designed to train the body's ability to produce force very quickly. While the notion of combining the physical training with skill work is sound, it is often impractical. Once an athlete leaves organized school programs, he spends long periods of time away from a coach who can guide them through skill training sessions. When this occurs, general physical abilities training can actually cause technical problems by creating bad habits when sport-specific skills are performed. One example that comes to mind is of a volleyball player who spent the summer away from her team because of an internship at a law firm. She did a lot of vertical jumps, box jumps and other general drills with a personal trainer and actually improved her vertical jump as measured during testing in training camp. Unfortunately, she had also picked up the habit of swinging her arms very vigorously to try to get more height on a jump. As a result, when she was jumping close to the net, she was constantly getting called for net fouls when her arms hit the net. It took almost half the season to break her of this habit and get her to have better control of her volleyball-specific jumping skills.

A Balanced Approach

As is often the case when developing training programs, if you are solely dedicated to one type of training, you are probably doing your athletes a disservice because the best training programs are an amalgamation of ideas. This is definitely the case when trying to decide to use specificity or general abilities training. In fact, the two schools of thought are actually much closer than most people think, particularly when accompanied by a good sport analysis. In fact in some cases, what may appear to be general training is actually specific training and vice versa, as this example demonstrates: Olympic weightlifters do little to no sprinting or jumping as part of their training yet there are many stories of weightlifters who, weighing over 300 lbs and being under six feet tall, can easily dunk a basketball or can sprint 10m faster than most sprinters. These abilities are due to their explosive training with very heavy weights, giving credence to the idea that training the ability to maximally recruit muscle fibers quickly is a general physical ability that improves performance in any skill requiring explosive power. At the same time, those who are proponents of specificity are quick to point out how closely the second pull phase of a clean or snatch is very similar in technique to a vertical jump.

So before deciding to favor one training philosophy over another, take a careful look at both and keep an open mind to the strengths and weaknesses that are inherent to any training methodology. We have always favored a mixed approach, based on a thorough analysis of the demands and movements of the sport and several general principles.

Sport Movement Analysis

A sport movement analysis is used to determine the muscles and movement patterns most commonly used in the sport. When done properly, this can be a very time-consuming process but, for those who make their living training athletes, it is a worthwhile investment that results in a very thorough understanding of the sport. The movement analysis is done using videos taken during games so that the frequency and type of activity used in game situations can most accurately be determined. The more videos used in the analysis, the better the analysis. However, time becomes a factor and sampling from 2-3 videos is usually enough to do an accurate analysis. The video used should be shot from above the playing area, using the stands or bleachers employing a wide enough angle to cover the whole playing area. Tapes of televised games will not work since the TV cameras follow the action rather than following an individual player or position eliminating the ability to analyze what is going on away from the play.

Conducting the Analysis

Once an acceptable tape is found it will need to be watched several times to identify everything you need to properly design the program.

Step 1: Select a Position

The movements and frequency with which they are used in a sport will vary from position to position. The movement analysis is done position by position so that the training program can be individualized to best meet the demands of the position.

Step 2: Conduct an Overview

The overview is designed to create a general feel for the demands of the sport. Many people spend their whole lives watching sports without ever getting an appreciation for the speed or physical demands of their sport. When you first review the tape, you need to review it as a scientist rather than a fan of the sport. Pay attention to the physicality of the sport and try to separate the skills from the fitness component. This is often more difficult than it sounds since skill and fitness are often linked. Look for major movements like jumping, sprinting, cutting, stopping, turning, etc. Are they performed explosively? In what direction does the athlete travel? Horizontal or vertical?

This overview often tells you right away whether you are going to need plyometrics or not. Sports that don't have very many bouts of explosive movement won't require plyos.

Step 3: Determine the Primary Movements

During the second review of the tape, you will be focusing on the primary movements. Again you will be identifying things like sprinting, jumping, stopping, cutting, turning, twisting, lunging and rotating, as well as direction (forward, backward, lateral, diagonal, vertical, horizontal), and whether they are done using one limb or both. Movements are different than skills, with skills being made up of movements. During the analysis, it is necessary to break the skill into its component movements. For instance a jump shot in basketball has the following movements: a stop and double-leg foot plant, a vertical jump, an extension of the shoulder to raise the arm overhead, and an extension of the forearm and wrist to shoot the ball. This level of analysis can help determine specific areas that require more physical conditioning and areas that need to focus on skill development.

Step 4: Determine the Frequency of the Primary Movements
Count the number of times each of the primary movements is performed. This will help determine the importance of different types of drill and exercises. The most frequent movements are the ones that deserve the most work. Often people focus on areas where they have the greatest weakness and, while it is important to overcome weaknesses, training to improve a weakness should not become the focus of training if the weakness occurs in a movement that is rarely used. For instance, if a running back has a weak throwing arm and has a tough time completing a half back option play, which the team uses 3-4 times per year, focusing on this skill will take away from training for the running back's primary functions and movements, not allowing him to improve the most important parts of his game. Once the frequency of primary movements has been determined, rank them from most to least frequently performed.

Step 4: Determine the Prime Mover Muscles Involved
This step will require some knowledge of anatomy and kinesiology but depending on how detailed you want to get in your analysis this does not have to be an in depth knowledge. Prime movers are those muscles that are responsible for making the movement happen. In the case of the jump portion of the jump shot the prime movers are the quadriceps, calves, glutes, and deltoids. As you watch the video be sure to pay attention to the movements because not all jumps are the same. Errors or insufficient analysis in step 3 will be compounded in this step by giving a false sense of what muscles are involved in the movement. For instance if an analysis were done on a ski jumper it would be easy to say that the movement is a vertical jump with the hands held at the sides. As you started to analyze the muscles involved you would think that the calves, quads, and glutes were the prime movers. However, if you look more closely at the jump in ski jumping you will notice that he calves are not involved because the feet need to stay flexed to keep the ski tips up to allow the jumper to maintain an aerodynamic position.

Step 5: Determine Antagonists and Stabilizers
Antagonists are those muscles that work opposite the prime movers. For instance, the hamstrings are the antagonist muscle group to the quadriceps. Antagonists act to stop a movement. In the case of plyometrics or other high-speed, high-power activities, they protect the joints from injury by slowing the movement near the end of the range of motion.

Stabilizers are those muscles that act to maintain body position or posture during a movement. They will often contract isometrically to do their job. The various muscles that make up the abdominal wall, including the internal and external obliques and rectus abdominus, are an example of common stabilizers that play a role in maintaining trunk posture during plyometric exercises. Stabilizers will act in pairs or groups surrounding a joint or set of joints.

Using the Analysis

Once you have done your sport analysis and know which muscles and movements need to be trained, you can start adding exercises to your program. There are a few guidelines that should be followed when constructing your yearly plan.

1. *General exercises under heavier load*
When using very heavy loads to develop maximum strength, the exercises should be general full-body multi-joint exercises, like squats.

2. *General exercises in the off-season*
The goals of off-season training are to prevent injury and develop a strength base that will allow you to do higher intensity plyos during the pre-season. Off-season training should focus on a variety of general exercises that work all the major muscle groups important to the sport, as well as antagonists and stabilizers.

3. *Specific exercises with game resistance*
When developing sport-specific power, speed of movement is the most important factor. Sport-specific movements should be done with resistances that are close to those used in the game. For instance, if you were training for golf, swinging a club that is a few grams heavier than your normal club will help improve club speed and driving distance. A club that is too heavy will change swing mechanics to the point that drive distance may actually decrease.

4. *Specific exercises during the season*
Sport-specific exercises, those that simulate all or part of the sport movement, are used during the season to maintain strength and transfer strength developed during the off-season to sport power. A basketball player may practice shooting with a light medicine ball to work on shot strength and power.

5. *Link specific exercises to skill training*
Power and strength are only useful when they improve an athlete's performance. Using actual sport skills to develop power will result in the best transfer of

training to performance. A volleyball player will get better transfer if he uses a volleyball approach into a vertical jump than he will if he performs a standing vertical jump. Whenever possible, skill and power training should be linked together.

Integrating Plyometrics With Other Workouts

A warm-up is the first component of any workout and is particularly important for plyometric training because of the maximal efforts required on every repetition. The type and goal of the workout will dictate the order of exercises. If the workout is focused solely on plyometrics, exercises will progress from low to high intensity, normally starting with double-leg single response jumps and progressing to double-leg multiple response jumps before moving on to single-leg activities, following the order outlined in Table 1.

If the workout combines skill and plyometric work, skill always takes priority. Without skill it is impossible to effectively use the fitness that you have developed, and as you move into higher and higher levels of competition this becomes more apparent. There are many examples of very fit athletes whose careers are very short because they lack the skill to play at the highest levels.

If plyometric and aerobic training are to be done in the same workout, the aerobic training should be relatively low intensity and done in the second half of the training session. Some people feel that doing the aerobic training first will provide a better warm-up for the plyometric training that follows. This may be true for relatively short aerobic training sessions of 20 minutes or less, but aerobic training will partially deplete the stores of carbohydrates in the muscles, robbing them of an important energy source for recovery between sets of plyometrics. Aerobic training uses predominantly slow-twitch muscle fibers. Slow-twitch fibers are not only used for long duration activity but they are the muscle fibers most responsible for posture and stability. If these fibers are fatigued prior to plyometric exercise, your ability to maintain proper body postures will be compromised, increasing the potential for injury.

Deciding the order of exercise becomes a little more complicated when strength training and plyometrics are combined into the same training session. This problem can be approached three ways, each of which has advantages and disadvantages depending upon individual situations.

Strength Before Plyometrics
Performing a strength training session prior to a plyometrics sessions will have a negative impact on the plyometrics session. Strength training and plyometrics both require a high level of nervous system activation. Fatigue from the strength session will decrease jump height and distance, decreasing the effectiveness of plyometric training. In addition, fatigued muscles will have more difficulty stopping the eccentric component of the plyometric exercise, increasing the amortization phase and decreasing the plyometric effect.

If plyometrics and strength training are done on the same day, try to alternate body regions between the workouts. For instance, if you do a lower body strength workout, the plyometric session should emphasize upper body throwing movements. If you do an upper body strength session, the plyometric workout should be lower body jump-based plyos.

Plyometrics Before Strength
Plyometrics before strength are less of a concern than strength before plyometrics. When plyos are done first, there will be some nervous system fatigue that could affect higher intensity strength training but hypertrophy-oriented workouts with moderate weight and moderate numbers of reps will not be affected by plyometric training.

Complex Training
Complex training, sometimes called contrast training, is a method of incorporating strength and plyometric training into the same workout. Training complexes can either be heavy/light or light/heavy, each of which has a specific training objective.

Heavy/Light Complex
A heavy/light complex involves performing a very heavy strength exercise followed by an explosive plyometric exercise. The heavy exercise stimulates the brain to maximally activate the muscle fibers. When the subsequent plyometric exercise is performed, the brain is still stimulated and there is an increase in the height or distance jumped. This is a good training method for those looking to increase their explosive power.

Light/Heavy Complex
A light/heavy complex involves performing 2-3 maximal jumps immediately before doing a heavy set of squats. The maximal jumps stimulate the nervous system and, if increasing the amount of weight used in the squat, increasing strength.

Regardless of the type of complex used, the first exercise is only done for 2-3 reps so that there is no fatigue that will affect the second exercise, which is the focus of the complex. If you find that the first exercise is not improving your performance. Then on the second exercise take a 2-3 minute rest between the two exercises. If this does not help then try increasing the intensity of the first exercise by using more weight or jumping higher.

Time of Day

The time of day can impact the order of exercise. Strength and power performance is greatest when body temperature is high. For most people, their normal 24-hour biological rhythm causes their body temperature to peak between 3 p.m. and 6 p.m. If possible, plyo training should be done during this time. If it isn't possible to train at this time, a longer warm-up will be necessary. If plyos are being combined with other forms of training first thing in the morning, plyos should be done half way through the training session when other activity has increased body temperature sufficiently.

Plyometrics are normally done during later stages of the training year. Once the individual's starting level has been determined, the program design is similar to that of strength training.

CHAPTER 5

PREPARATORY DRILLS AND EXERCISES

The drills and exercises described in this chapter are used in the Level 1 and Level 2 programs to prepare the athlete for full sport-specific plyometric programs. They are designed to teach basic body movements and control. Some of the drills, like forward running, are self explanatory and not included in this chapter. Others, like the medicine ball tosses, are included in other chapters.

Swiss Ball Partner Perturbations

Stand with feet shoulder with a part, holding a Swiss ball at arm's length in front of you. Your partner is standing opposite you. Once you have a firm grip on the ball, your partner will start hitting it, trying to hit it upwards, downwards, diagonally, and laterally. You must maintain your grip on the ball with feet still.

Single-leg Tennis Ball Toss

Stand on one foot, holding a tennis ball in one hand. Toss the tennis ball to a partner. Maintaining your balance on one foot, have your partner toss the ball back. Initially, tosses will be right back to you so that they are easy to catch. After several sessions of this drill, the ball should be tossed high, low and to the side so that the person receiving the ball has to stretch and bend to catch the ball. Balance on one foot must be maintained at all times.

Single-leg Medicine Ball Pick Ups

Stand on one leg and with a medicine ball on the ground beside you. Rotating from the hips and maintaining your balance on one leg bend over and pick up the medicine ball. As you get better at this drill, move the medicine ball farther away from your body.

Walking Lunges

Walking lunges require enough space for you to take 6-8 long walking strides. Hold a dumbbell in each hand or place a barbell across the back of the shoulders. Your feet are shoulder width apart. Keeping the torso upright, take a long step forward with one leg, allowing the front leg to bend to 90°. The back leg should be slightly bent. Shift your weight onto the front leg and stand back up, bringing the back leg forward. Step forward again, leading with the other leg. Continue this long striding motion for the prescribed number of repetitions.

Lateral Lunges

Place a bar in a squat rack and dip under the bar, positioning the bar across the shoulders at the top of the posterior deltoid with the load distributed across the back. Place your hands just outside your shoulders. Keep your head up, chest out, and shoulders back. Your back should be flat with a slight arch at the base; feet are shoulder width apart.

Take two long steps backward out of the rack and reset your feet so that they are shoulder width apart. Take a long step directly sideways with one leg, shifting your weight onto that leg and bending it until the top of your thigh is parallel to the ground. The other leg will be straight with the whole foot in contact with the ground. Press the lead foot into the ground and push yourself back to an upright standing position. Repeat the same movement with the other leg leading.

Inch Worms

Lie face down in a push-up position with thumbs aligned just under your shoulders. Keeping your arms and legs straight, slowly start walking your feet toward your hands, raising your rear end up into the air. When you have brought your feet as close to your hands as possible, while keeping legs and arms straight, walk your hands forward and lower your body back to the push-up position.

Step Up

The box or bench used for this exercise needs to be high enough to create a 120-degree angle at the knee when the foot is placed on the box. Hold a dumbbell in each hand or place a barbell across the back of your shoulders as you would in the squat, feet are shoulder width apart, head is up, your chest is out and shoulders are back. Stand 12-18 inches behind the box or bench. Place the entire foot of one leg on the top of the box, shifting your weight to the leg on the box. Powerfully extend the knee, hip, and ankle of the foot on the box, and bring your body to a standing position on top of the box. Step off the box, keeping all your weight on your working leg and lightly touch the ground with the non-working leg, do not put any weight on the non-working leg, because it is only being used as a guide to tell you when you have gone low enough. Immediately stand back up. Keep your trunk upright throughout the movement; avoid bending over at the waist.

Box Drill

The box drill is designed to improve the ability to cut or round corners. In order to attain these goals, it is important to understand the different types of directional changes:

CUTTING involves an abrupt change of direction.

CORRECT CUT	INCORRECT CUT
wide base	narrow base
athletic position; stay low	standing straight up
on balance, shoulders over hips	off balance, leaning over

ROUNDING a corner involves maintaining speed while changing direction or turning.

CORRECT ROUND	INCORRECT ROUND
base narrow	base wide
quick, choppy feet	slow, long steps
fast arm action	slow arm action

THE ATHLETIC POSITION is feet spread apart, knees bent, and the shoulders/hips over the feet in order to maintain balance. This is the optimal position for performing almost all sport movements.

In the box drill four cones are laid out in a square. The athlete starts at one corner and sprints as fast as possible to the next corner, cutting or rounding the corner. The type of corner should be alternated with each repeat of the drill. Make sure that the drill is done both clockwise and counterclockwise.

Lateral High Knee Hurdles

Set up the hurdles in a straight line with about 60cm between hurdles. Have the athlete start with the hurdles on their side. The athlete will sidestep over the hurdles as fast as possible. Stay in a good athletic position as you move laterally through the drill. Maintain efficient arm action by keeping the elbows bent at 90 degrees, driving them back and forth. Keep the head up and eyes looking forward throughout the drill.

Forward High Knee Hurdles

Set up the hurdles in a straight line with about 60cm between each hurdle. The athlete will run in a straight line over the hurdles placing one foot between each hurdle. Focus on correct posture and maximal effort. Concentrate on driving the knees high for maximal hip flexion. Maintain efficient arm action by keeping the elbows bent at 90 degrees, driving them forward and back. Keep the head up and eyes looking forward throughout the drill.

Swiss Ball Seated Balance

Choose a stability ball that will allow there to be a 90-degree angle at the knee when seated. Sit upright on the ball with shoulders back and chest out, don't slouch. Keep your feet away from the ball and raise one leg so that it is parallel to the floor. Hold for 15 seconds, lower the leg and repeat with the other leg.

Skating Position Single-Leg Tennis Ball Toss

This drill is identical to the single-leg tennis ball toss except that the supporting leg is bent slightly and your trunk is inclined forward, putting you into a body position similar to that used during ice skating. Maintaining your balance on one foot, have your partner toss the ball back. Initially, tosses will be right back to you so that they are easy to catch. After several sessions of this drill, the ball should be tossed high, low and to the side so that the person receiving the ball has to stretch and bend to catch the ball. Balance on one foot must be maintained at all times.

Medicine Ball Squats

Hold a medicine ball straight in front of you at arm's length. Point your toes outward at an angle of 30-35°. Inhale deeply and contract the muscles of the torso to help stabilize your upper body and keep your back flat. Descend by slowly lowering the buttocks toward the floor, keeping your hips under the bar as much as possible. Descend until the tops of the thighs are parallel to the floor. The ascent starts with a powerful drive to accelerate the weight out of the bottom position. Keep your head looking up to help counter leaning forward. Keep the muscles of your torso contracted throughout the ascent phase of the lift. Continue to push with your legs until you come to a full standing position. Take another deep breath and descend for the next rep.

Clock Lunges

Place a bar in a squat rack and dip under the bar, positioning the bar across the shoulders at the top of the posterior deltoid with the load distributed across the back. Place your hands just outside your shoulders. Keep your head up, chest out, and shoulders back. Your back should be flat with a slight arch at the base; feet are shoulder width apart.

Take two long steps backward out of the rack and reset your feet so that they are shoulder width apart. Take a step straight forward with your right foot, where the 12 would be on a clock, landing heel first, shifting your weight from heel to toes. Continue to bend the right leg until the top of you thigh is parallel to the ground. The left leg should bend until it is about one inch above the ground. Press the heel of the right leg into the ground and push yourself back to an upright standing position. While continuing to face straight ahead, step forward and slightly to the right, placing your foot on the 1 of a clock face. Step back and repeat for 2, 3, 4, 5, and 6 o'clock all with the right foot. When stepping to 4 and 5 o'clock, you will be stepping backwards and slightly sideways so be careful about the balance in these steps. Once you have completed all the steps with the right foot the left foot will do 12, 11, 10, 9, 8, 7, and 6 o'clock.

Crossover Step Up

The box or bench used for this exercise needs to be high enough to create a 120 degree angle at the knee when the foot is placed on the box. Hold a dumbbell in each hand or place a barbell across the back of your shoulders as you would in the squat, feet are hip width apart, head is up, your chest is out and shoulders are back. Stand 12-18 inches to one side of the box or bench. Cross one leg in front of the other and place the entire foot of the leg that has crossed on the top of the box, shifting your weight to the leg on the box. Powerfully extend the knee, hip, and ankle of the foot on the box, and bring your body to a standing position on top of the box. Step off the box, keeping all your weight on your working leg and lightly touch the ground with the non-working leg. Do not put any weight on the non-working leg because it is only being used as a guide to tell you when you have gone low enough. Immediately stand back up. When you have completed all the repetitions for one leg, move to the other side of the box and repeat the exercise for the other leg. Keep your trunk upright throughout the movement; avoid bending over at the waist.

Board Stepping

Board stepping helps improve balance during changes of direction. Place foot-sized flat boards or another form of a flat target on the ground in a random pattern. The boards should be close enough together so that you can step from one to another with a long step. Start on one board and step to the next, moving forwards, backward and laterally. When you are comfortable with board stepping, difficulty can be increased by spacing the boards farther apart so that you have to hop from one board to another. Another more difficult alternative is to toss and catch a tennis or medicine ball while stepping from board to board.

Ladder Forward, Backward and Lateral Run Series

Begin by standing at one end of the ladder in one of three positions; facing the ladder, with your back to the ladder, or sideways. Start in a sport ready position and enter the first rung with either foot. Place both feet in each box, one at a time. The goal is to do this consistently in each rung with the head up, rapid arm action, and while maintaining the sport position throughout the drill. There is a tendency to lead with one foot, but in athletics it is disadvantageous to favor either side. Thus, practice the drill leading with both feet. Maintain center of balance over the feet so you do not fall forward or off to either side.

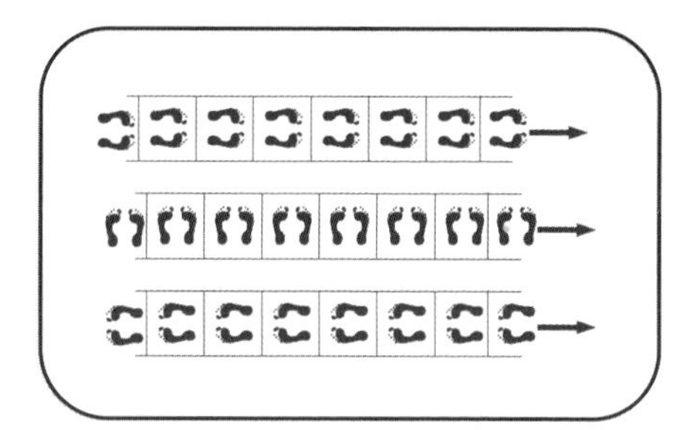

Tubing Overhead Press

Place the exercise tube under your feet and hold a piece of tubing in each hand so that the handles are at waist height. Grasping the handles in an overhand grip, bring them to shoulder height so that your palms face away from your body. Keep your head up, chest out, and shoulders back. Your back should be flat with a slight arch at the base; feet are shoulder width apart. Press the handles overhead until your arms are fully extended. Bend the elbows and control the handles back down to the shoulders and the starting position.

Swiss Ball Walkouts

Kneel in back of a Swiss ball, chest against the ball. Place your hands on the ground in front of the ball and roll onto the ball. Continue to roll forward, walking out onto your hands until only your shins are on the ball. Be sure to keep your body flat throughout the movement by tightening your abdominal muscles.

Ladder Icky Shuffle

Begin with the left foot in the first box and the right foot to the outside of the ladder. The first step is to bring the right foot into the first box. The next step is to take the left foot and step up to the outside of the second box. Then bring the right foot directly into the second box. Then bring the left foot into the box next to the right foot. This process should then be repeated with the right foot leading the next step.

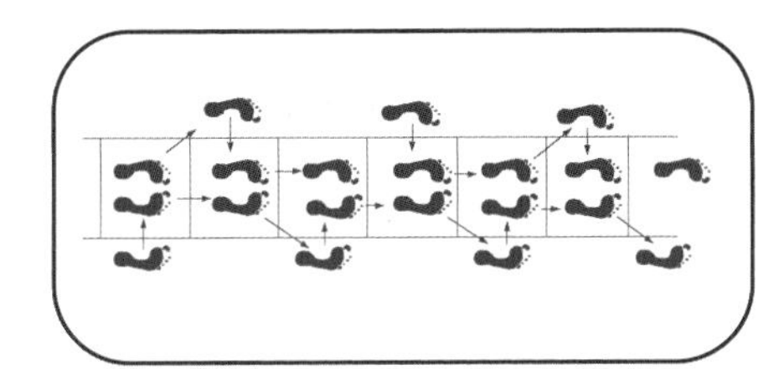

Ladder Buzz Saws

Start on the outside of the ladder on the right or left side, facing the ladder. Then put the right foot in followed by the left foot. The next step is to advance the right foot up to the outside of the ladder followed by the left foot.

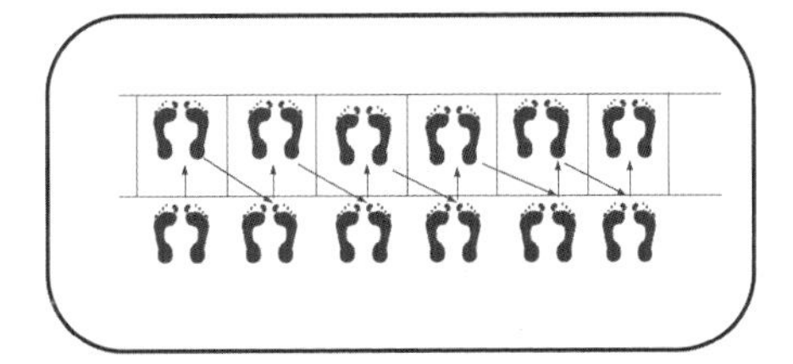

Hurdle Two Foot Hops

Set up the hurdles in a straight line with 60cm between hurdles. Have the athlete hop over the hurdles as fast as possible while keeping the feet together and touching the ground at the same time. Ground time should be minimized between each jump.

Tubing Partner Rows

Sit on the floor with legs straight in front. Have your partner hold one end of the tubing or loop the tubing around your feet. Then sit upright and grasp the handles with a narrow overhand grip. Your legs are straight and your back is flat. Bending forward from the hips about 20 degrees, pull the handles toward your body by straightening the back. Once the handle reaches your knees, use the arm to finish the pull and bring the handle to the base of your sternum.

Power Sled Push and Drag

Load a power sled with the required weight. Stand behind the sled and bend over to grasp the handles. With straight arms, start sprinting, pushing the sled in front of you. The sled can also be pulled or dragged by attaching a harness to yourself and the sled.

Power sled push and drag

Up and Back

Place two cones 10 yards apart. Start at one cone and sprint to the second cone. Break and come to a complete stop in a good athletic position. Make a quick turn and accelerate in the opposite direction. Sprint past the starting point. Focus on maintaining body weight balanced over the feet and changing directions as fast as possible.

T-Drill

Set four cones in a T with 3m between cones. Starting at the base of the T, sprint forward to the middle cone, shuffle laterally to one of the outside cones, shuffle all the way back across to the other outside cone, shuffle back to the center cone and backpedal to the base cone.

M-Drill

Set five cones in an M pattern with 3m between cones. Sprint forward from the first cone to the second. Backpedal laterally to the next cone, sprint forward and laterally to the fourth cone and backpedal to the final cone

Star-Drill

Lay five cones out on the ground, four forming a square with the corners 3m apart and the fifth in the center of the square. Starting in an athletic ready position, run forward and diagonally to touch the first corner, backpedal to the center and run forward to the other corner, back pedal to the center. Backpedal to one of the back corners and run forwards to the center repeat for the final corner.

Partner Resisted Sprints

Two people with comparable speed are paired up for this drill. One wears a belt with sprint resistor tubing attached, the other holds the loose end tightly. The tubing should be taut, with little slack. It is important to keep constant tension on the tubes but not overstretch them. Begin with one partner lined up in front of the other. The partner in front starts to run. When he has gone about 5 yards, the other partner starts to follow at a slightly slower pace so that the tubing continues to stretch and the resistance increases. As this is a physically taxing drill, short distances of 15-30 yards are run.

Focus on correct posture and maximal effort at all times. Maintain an upright body alignment while sprinting; do not bend at the waist. Concentrate on driving the knees high for maximal hip flexion and fully extending the hips to increase stride length. Maintain efficient arm action by keeping the elbows bent at 90 degrees at all times and driving them straight forward and back.

Two Person Get Up and React

Two people lie flat on the back, knees bent so that feet are on the ground. A third person stands 10m away with a tennis ball in one hand. When the person with the ball says go, the other two get up and start to sprint toward the person with the ball. The ball is thrown and the two people running react and race to catch the ball.

Partner Resisted Lateral Shuffles

Two people with comparable speed are paired up for this drill. One wears a belt with sprint resistor tubing attached, the other holds the loose end tightly. The tubing should be taut, with little slack. It is important to keep constant tension on the tubes but not overstretch them. Begin with one partner standing beside the other.

The partner wearing the tubing starts to side shuffle, keeping his feet under his hips so that their feet do not come together, hips are low, head is up and chest is out. When he has gone about 5 yards, the other partner starts to jog toward him at a slightly slower pace so that the tubing continues to stretch and the resistance increases. As this is a physically taxing drill, short distances of 15-30 yards are run. Focus on correct posture and maximal effort at all times.

CHAPTER 6

UPPER BODY PLYOMETRIC EXERCISES

Overhead Throw

Hold a medicine ball overhead in both hands, feet shoulder width apart, knees slightly flexed. Bend backwards slightly, shifting your weight onto your toes and allowing your trunk to incline back. At the same time, lower the medicine ball behind your head by bending at the elbows and extending the shoulders. Explosively drive your hips backward, straightening your body and arms at the same time, bending at the waist, throwing the ball as far forward as possible. The momentum of the arm and hip should pull you forward, causing you to bend over at the waist. Start with a 1-2 lb medicine ball or a basketball until you are comfortable with the movement sequence and timing.

Kneeling Two-hand Overhead Throw

This drill is identical to the overhead throw except it is done from a kneeling position, decreasing the involvement of the trunk and legs. This drill can be done with a partner who throws the ball back as soon as he catches it, minimizing the time of possession of the ball.

Kneeling Overhead Throw

Seated Two-hand Overhead Throw

Another overhead throw progression that further isolates the musculature of the shoulders and arms. Sit in a solid, stable chair and hold the medicine ball in both hands overhead. Bend the elbows and flex the shoulders to create a pre-stretch and then explosively throw the ball as far as possible. Keep your back against the chair at all times to minimize trunk muscle involvement.

Soccer Throw-in

Hold a medicine ball overhead in both hands, feet about hip width apart. Take a large, explosive step forward and throw the ball as far as possible. Your arms will bend slightly at the elbow allowing both the upper arms and shoulders to be involved in the throw. There will also be a slight backwards bend on the trunk when you step forward, stretching the trunk muscles, allowing them to contribute to the throw.

Medicine Ball Chest Pass

Stand with feet shoulder width apart, and hold a medicine ball in front of you at arms length, keeping your arms parallel to the ground. Rapidly bend at the elbows, bringing the ball toward your chest. When the ball is 3-4 inches away from your chest, quickly reverse direction and push the ball away from you rapidly, throwing it as far and as fast as possible. This drill can be done keeping the feet shoulder width apart for the whole drill, which places a greater emphasis on the upper body or you can add a forward step, making it similar to a chest pass used in basketball, involving the trunk and hips.

Seated Chest Pass

The seated chest pass is similar to the standing chest pass only it isolates the muscles of the upper body more effectively. Sit on the ground with your back against a wall or sit in a chair. Hold a medicine ball in front of you at arm's length, keeping your arms parallel to the ground. Rapidly bend at the elbows, bringing the ball toward your chest. When the ball is 3-4 inches away from your chest, quickly reverse direction and push the ball away from yourself rapidly, throwing it as far and as fast as possible.

Rapid Fire Chest Pass

This drill can be done from either a standing or seated position. Stand across from a partner with feet shoulder width apart, hold a medicine ball in front of you at arm's length, keeping your arms parallel to the ground. Rapidly bend at the elbows, bringing the ball toward your chest. When the ball is 3-4 inches away from your chest quickly reverse direction and push the ball away from you rapidly, throwing it as hard and as fast as possible. As soon as your partner catches the ball, he will throw it back to you. The objective is to have the ball in your hands for as short a period of time as possible. Try to get as many throws as possible in 15 seconds before taking a break. If you are using a medicine ball that bounces, this drill can be done against a wall instead of with a partner.

Rapid Fire Chest Pass

Supine Power Drop

A partner and box are needed for this drill. Lie on your back with your head near the plyo box, knees are bent, feet are flat on the floor, arms are extended straight over your chest and the hands are in position to catch a ball. Your partner will stand on the box and hold a ball directly over your hands. The ball is dropped. As soon as it is caught, absorb the impact as quickly as possible and throw it back up to the person on the box. It is important for both people to make good throws so that a rhythm can be established. This drill often works better with two balls and three people. The third person is responsible for catching the throw from the person on the ground and handing the ball to the person on the box. As everyone becomes more comfortable with the drill, the person on the box can throw the ball down rather than dropping it, increasing the force that needs to be absorbed and the pre-stretch.

Supine Power Drop

Seated Power Drop

A partner and box are needed for this drill. Sit with your back against a box, legs straight in front of you, arms extended overhead and just in front of your face, in a position similar to that used in volleying a volleyball. Your partner will stand on the box and hold a ball directly over your hands. The ball is dropped and as soon as it is caught, absorb the impact as quickly as possible and throw it back up to the person on the box. It is important for both people to make good throws so that a rhythm can be established. Again, a third person will improve the rhythm of this drill.

Seated Power Drop

Partner Drop Push-ups

From a kneeling position, keep your trunk straight as a partner holds onto your shoulders. Keeping a straight line from your shoulders to your knees, start to lean forward while your partner holds you back. Once your trunk gets to about a 60° angle, your partner will let go, allowing you to fall to the floor. Catch yourself with your hands, absorbing the impact as rapidly as possible and turning the momentum around by pushing yourself off the floor as explosively as possible. When first starting this drill, your partner can hold on until you are closer to the floor.

Depth Drop Push-up

Two low boxes, 4-8 inches high, are needed. Start in the up position of a push-up with hands on the boxes slightly wider than shoulder width. Slide your hands off the boxes and fall to the floor. Catch yourself on your hands, absorb the impact as quickly as possible and push yourself back up onto the boxes. The boxes should be supported so that they don't slide or move when your hands land on them.

Clap Push-ups

Assume the top position of a push-up. Hands just outside your shoulders, feet together back flat, face pointed at the floor. Rapidly descend into the bottom position. When your chest is 2-3 inches from the ground, reverse your direction and push yourself up as quickly as possible. Try to accelerate yourself all the way through the push-up so that your hands leave the ground when you reach the top. Clap your hands together, catch yourself and repeat for the required number of repetitions. It is essential to keep your abs tight and back flat throughout this drill. Any sagging of the trunk or shoulders will make it more difficult to get off the ground and increase your chance of injury.

Standing Toss for Height

Stand holding a medicine ball with straight arms near your waist. Keep your feet shoulder width apart. Keeping the arms straight, squat down slightly, allowing your trunk to incline and throw the ball as high as possible. Keep the feet on the ground so that the majority of the power for the throw comes from the arms, with the legs only providing an assist. This drill can be done with a medicine ball or a throwing weight.

Kneeling Toss for Height

This drill is similar to the underhand toss for height but is done from a kneeling position. Hold a medicine ball with straight arms at waist height. Kneel on the ground or a mat so that there is a straight line from the shoulders through to the knees. Bend forward from the waist until the ball almost touches the ground, drive the hips forward and up while swinging the arms overhead, throwing the ball as high as possible with straight arms.

Seated Toss for Height

This drill is similar to the underhand toss for height but done from a seated position. Hold a medicine ball with straight arms at waist height. Sit on the ground or a mat, keeping the chest out and shoulders back so that the back stays flat.

Bend forward slightly from the hips, keeping the back flat until the ball almost touches the ground. Take a deep breath and contract your abs to stabilize your trunk. Rapidly straighten your trunk while driving the arms overhead, throwing the ball as high as possible with straight arms. The trunk will contribute very little to this throw, so a lighter ball than in the preceding two drills should be used.

Two-hand Side Throw

This drill is similar to the overhead throw, only the ball is thrown to the side of the head rather than over the head. Hold a medicine ball overhead in both hands, feet shoulder width apart, knees slightly flexed. Bend backwards slightly, shifting your weight onto your toes and allowing your trunk to incline back.

At the same time, lower the medicine ball behind your head by bending at the elbows and extending the shoulders. Explosively drive your hips backward, straightening your body and arms at the same time, bending at the waist, throwing the ball as far forward as possible. The momentum of the arm and hip drive should pull you forward, causing you to bend over at the waist. Both arms must stay involved in the throw or you risk injuring your shoulder.

Heavy Bag Chest Throw

Stand in front of a heavy bag. About 12 inches from the bag, in an athletic stance, place one foot slightly in front of the other, squatted low so that your hands are near the bottom of the bag. Place both hands on the bag and push it out as hard as possible. When the bag swings back, absorb the impact as quickly as possible and explosively press it out again. A fairly heavy bag is needed for this drill. If the bag is too light, it becomes possible to stop the bag very quickly with minimal absorption and pre-stretch, decreasing the plyometric effect.

One-arm Heavy Bag Push

Stand to the side of a heavy bag, one foot in front of the other in a stance similar to that you would have when throwing a baseball, squatted down so that your hand will be on the lower quarter of the bag. When hanging still, the edge of the bag should be in line with your shoulder. Place one hand in the middle of the bag, near the bottom. Using a trunk rotation and arm drive, push the bag away from you as explosively as possible. As the bag swings back, catch it in the same hand, quickly absorbing the impact using both the arm and a trunk rotation and then throw it out again.

Ball Slams

A fully inflated rubber medicine ball that bounces should be used. Hold the medicine ball overhead in both hands, feet shoulder width apart, knees slightly flexed. Bend backwards slightly, shifting your weight onto your toes and allowing your trunk to incline back. At the same time, lower the medicine ball behind your head by bending at the elbows and extending the shoulders. Explosively drive your hips backward, straightening your body and arms at the same time, bending at the waist, slamming the ball onto the ground as hard as possible. Use a level field or floor for this drill so that the ball is easier to catch. It is a good idea to have high ceilings if doing this drill indoors so that the ball doesn't damage anything.

Ball Slams

Finger Rolls

Finger Rolls

Stand with feet shoulder width apart, arms at your side with a Power Throw Ball in one hand, palm up. Bend you elbow to 90° so that your forearm is parallel to the ground. Holding the ball just on your fingers, flick it as high as possible.

Reverse Wrist Toss

Stand with feet shoulder width apart, arms at your side with a Power Throw Ball in one hand, palm down. Bend you elbow to 90° so that your forearm is parallel to the ground. Bend your wrist as far down as possible. Rapidly extend your wrist and flip the ball to your partner using only your wrist, not moving any other part of your arm. This drill can also be done from a kneeling position

Reverse Wrist Toss

Lateral Triceps Toss

Lateral Triceps Toss

Stand with feet should width apart, Power Throw Ball in one hand. Raise your arm to the side so that it is at shoulder height, parallel to the ground. Keeping your arm parallel to the ground, bend your elbow, bringing your hand as close to your body as possible. Reverse direction as quickly as possible, straighten your arm and toss the ball to the side.

Overhead Triceps Toss

Hold a Power Grip Ball in one hand arm straight overhead. Bend your arm so that your elbow is perpendicular to the ground, pointing straight upward. The ball should be just behind your head. Straighten your arm as quickly as possible and toss the ball into the air using only your triceps.

CHAPTER 7

LOWER BODY PLYOMETRIC EXERCISES

Double Leg Jumps

Standing Vertical Jump

This drill will help teach learning mechanics and serves as an introductory level exercise. Single vertical jumps can be used even if the athlete has not achieved the strength goals outlined in the chapter on getting started.

Stand with feet about shoulder width apart. Swing the arms back and quickly dip until the knees bend to about 120 degrees. Explode upward extending the knees, hips, ankles and trunk while swinging the arms forward and upward as explosively as possible.

Focus on completely extending the body, reaching as high as possible. The arm drive is critical for achieving maximum jump height. This drill can be done under a basketball net or backboard so that the athlete can monitor his progress and consistency of his jumps.

Standing Vertical Jump

Countermovement Squat Jump

The squat jump is similar to the vertical jump but it does not incorporate an arm drive. Stand with feet shoulder width apart, hands are positioned behind the head with fingers entwined. Quickly dip until the knees are bent to about 120 degrees. Explode upwards by rapidly extending the knees, hips, ankles and trunk. The height achieved in the squat jump will be less than that of the vertical jump. As an alternative to hands behind the head, a short rope can be held behind the back.

Static Squat Jump

The set up and positioning for the static squat jump are the same as that of the countermovement squat jump. Instead of dipping rapidly squat down until the top of the thighs are just about parallel to the floor. Without dipping lower, explode upward by rapidly extending the hips, knees, ankles and trunk. This drill is particularly beneficial for athletes who have not achieved the strength goals outlined in the getting started chapter as it places a greater emphasis on strength development, especially starting strength, and less on the rebound effect from the elastic component of the muscle.

Tuck Jump

Tuck Jump

This is an excellent drill for improving hip flexor strength and speed. The hip flexors are used extensively during sprinting activities. Assume the same starting position as in the vertical jump. Swing the arms back and jump as high as possible, extending the knees, hips, ankles and trunk. While in the air, quickly pull the knees into the chest, grabbing them with both hands prior to landing.

Butt Kick Jumps

Stand with feet about shoulder width apart. Swing the arms back and quickly dip until the knees bend to about 120 degrees. Explode upward extending the knees, hips, ankles and trunk while swinging the arms forward and upward as explosively as possible. Focus on completely extending the body, reaching as high as possible. At the top of the jump, kick the feet back so that the heels touch your buttocks. Straighten the legs and land.

Butt Kick Jump

Pike Jump

Pike Jump

Stand with feet about shoulder width apart. Swing the arms back and quickly dip until the knees bend to about 120 degrees. Explode upward extending the knees, hips, ankles and trunk while swinging the arms forward and upward as explosively as possible. At the same time, the legs are vigorously swung forward so that they are parallel to the floor while you reach forward trying to touch your toes.

Box Landing

This drill teaches landing technique and should be used prior to starting any other box jumps. The box should be high enough that the knees don't bend any more than 120° during the landing. After stepping up, stand on the box with feet shoulder width apart. Step off the box and land with both feet, absorbing the landing in as short a period of time as possible by landing on the balls of the feet, bending the knees and slightly inclining the trunk. While it can be used by everyone as a means of teaching landing, this is a particularly effective drill for gymnasts and figure skaters who are required to stick a landing.

Box Landing

Box Jump

This drill requires a box or set of boxes, varying in height from 60-145cm. The boxes should be solidly built with a non-slip landing surface. Stand facing the box with feet hip width to shoulder width apart, about an arm's length away from the box. Dip rapidly, swing the arms driving them upwards and jump onto the box. Jump just high enough to land on the box in a half squat position. Return to the ground by stepping down or hopping off the box.

Speed Box Jumps

The objective of this drill is to repeat 5-10 jumps as quickly as possible. The equipment and positioning are the same as in the box jump. Jump up so that the front half of the foot lands on the box. As soon as the feet land on the box pull them off and land on the ground. Repeat the jump immediately after landing. Try not to push off the box when returning to the ground as this will move you farther away from the box, making the next jump more difficult.

High Knee Box Jump

This drill requires a box or set of boxes, varying in height from 60-145cm. The boxes should be solidly built with a non-slip landing surface. Stand facing the box with feet hip width to shoulder width apart, about an arms length away from the box. Dip rapidly, swing the arms driving them upwards and jump onto the box, landing in a deep squat position. While in the air, the knees should be quickly brought toward the chest as in the tuck jump. This will help increase speed and strength in the hip flexors, which is necessary for improving running

High Knee Box Jump

speed. Box height will be higher than in the box jump due to the deep squat landing. Some athletes will become apprehensive as box height increases. It may be necessary to attach a mat or pad to the front of the box to alleviate their fear of jumping into the box.

Box Jump and Leap

This is an advanced drill that must be performed with a soft landing surface. This drill requires a box or set of boxes, varying in height from 60-145cm. The boxes should be solidly built with a non-slip landing surface. Stand facing the box with feet hip width to shoulder width apart, about an arm's length away from the box. Dip rapidly, swing the arms, driving them upwards and jump onto the box. As soon as you land on the box, leap forward as far as possible, landing on the ground and absorbing the impact as quickly as possible.

Box Jump and Leap

Box to Box Jump

The box to box jump is a form of depth jump. Stand on a box, feet shoulder width apart, hands at your sides. Step off the box. As soon as you land on the ground, stop yourself and jump onto a second box. The height of the second box is the same or greater than the first box. This drill can be made more difficult by turning it into a multiple response drill, using a series of 3-5 progressively higher boxes. The boxes should be 36-40 inches apart so that there is adequate space to land and swing the arms for the second jump without fear of hitting a box.

Depth Jump

Depth jumps are very advanced plyometrics exercises. Athletes weighing more than 110kg (240 lbs) are at increased risk of injury from depth jumps and should only use depth jumps if they can squat at least twice their body weight. Start by standing on a box, feet shoulder width apart, hands at your sides. Step off the box. As soon as you land on the ground stop yourself and jump as high as possible. The maximum box height is one that still allows you

to jump higher when you step off the box than you could if you did a standing vertical jump. Try several different heights until you find the maximum height that you can effectively use. Be sure to step off the box rather than jump off the box, jumping off the box can add unnecessary height to the drill, making it more difficult to select the right box height and monitor progress.

Depth Jump and Leap

Set up as for the depth jump but jump forward as far as possible rather than jumping for height upon landing. This drill is best done into a sand pit or other very soft landing area so that the legs can be swung forward upon landing, maximizing jump distance.

Depth Jump and Sprint

This is a particularly good drill for rugby, soccer, basketball and any other sport where the athlete is required to accelerate into a sprint upon landing. Use the same height box that you would use for depth jumps. Start by standing on a box, feet shoulder width apart,

Depth Jump and Sprint

Depth Jump and Side Step

hands at your sides. Step off the box. As soon as you land on the ground, sprint forward as fast as possible for 10 yards. Focus on accelerating to maximum speed as quickly as possible. The first step out of the landing will be a short double-leg hop forward to transfer your weight and momentum from the vertical landing to a horizontal sprint motion.

Depth Jump and Side Step

This version of the depth jump is particularly good for volleyball and basketball players because it creates similar demands to what will be seen in a game situation where it is necessary to move quickly following a landing. Set up and performance of this drill is identical to the depth jump but upon landing there is an explosive lateral side step rather than a jump for height. Try to cover as much distance as quickly as possible with the side step.

Stadium Leaps

Start at the bottom of a set of sturdy stadium steps. Stand with feet shoulder width apart. Swing the arms back and quickly dip until the knees bend to about 120 degrees. Explode upward extending the knees, hips, ankles and trunk while swinging the arms forward and upward as explosively as possible. Focus on completely extending the body, reaching as high as possible. Jumping two steps at a time leap until you reach the top of the stadium or complete 10 jumps. The steps must be wide enough to land full foot, and sturdy enough to absorb the impact of heavy athletes. Care must be taken in the last 2-3 jumps of each set to ensure a solid landing. As fatigue sets in, jump height decreases, increasing the chance of falling on the steps.

Standing Long Jump

Stand with feet about shoulder width apart. Swing the arms back and quickly dip until the knees bend to about 120 degrees. Explode forward extending the knees, hips, ankles and trunk while swinging the arms forward and upward as explosively as possible. Focus on completely extending the body, reaching as high as possible. Swing the legs forward and land heels first, absorbing the impact with your legs, to maximize jumping distance. Single jumps should be done into a sand pit or onto a well padded landing mat.

Multiple Long Jump

Not to be confused with a hop, this is a maximal effort drill where you are attempting to jump as far as possible on each jump. The starting position is the same as the standing long jump. Upon landing, shift your weight back onto the front half of your feet and immediately jump again. Spend as little time as possible in the transition from one jump to the next. This drill can also be done without swinging the arms, holding a piece of rope in both hands behind your back to help isolate the legs and hips.

Hurdle Hops

8-10 low hurdles, 8-15 inches high, are needed for this drill. Space the hurdles about 18-24 inches apart. Stand facing the hurdles with feet hip width apart, hands at the sides. Hop over the first hurdle, hopping just high enough to clear the hurdle. As soon as you land, hop over the second hurdle and continue this pattern until all hurdles have been cleared. The objective of this drill is to clear all the hurdles as fast as possible without hitting any of them. Keep the feet hip width apart throughout the whole drill, resisting the temptation to step over the hurdle. If hurdles are not available, low benches or cones can substitute.

Hurdle Hops

Lateral Hurdle Hops

Lateral Hurdle Hops

Performed like the hurdle hops, set up a series of hurdles in a straight line. Begin with the ladder line on the side of the athlete. Hop sideways over the hurdles extending the knees, hips, and ankles while swinging the arms upwards. Try to keep the hips perpendicular to the hurdles, there may be a tendency to rotate the hips to make the hops easier. Again, during this drill the focus should be on decreasing ground contact time. Maintain an athletic sport position throughout.

Reverse Hurdle Hops

Set up a straight line of hurdles like in the forward and lateral hurdle drills. This time the athlete will start with the line of hurdles directly behind himself. A backwards jump will be performed over the first hurdle. To perform this jump, extend the knees, ankles, and hips while swinging the arms upward. After landing, repeat this process. During this drill the focus should be on decreasing ground contact time. Maintain an athletic sport position throughout.

Reverse Hurdle Hops

Hurdle Jumps

4-5 high hurdles, 24-40 inches high, are needed for this drill. Space the hurdles about 18-24 inches apart. Stand facing the hurdles with feet hip width apart, hands at the sides. Jump over the first hurdle, jumping just high enough to clear the hurdle. As soon as you land, hop over the second hurdle and continue this pattern until all hurdles have been cleared. Knees will have to be quickly brought toward the just as in the high knee box jump to allow you to clear higher hurdles. The objective of this drill is to clear all the hurdles as fast as possible without hitting any of them. Keep the feet hip width apart throughout the whole drill. The hurdles can all be the same height or they can progress from low to high.

Lateral Jumps

The objective of this drill is to jump as far sideways as possible, taking off and landing on both feet. Start with feet hip width apart. Swing the arms back and quickly dip until the knees bend to about 120 degrees. Explode upward and sideways extending the knees, hips, ankles and trunk while swinging the arms forward and slightly sideways as explosively as possible. Jumps need to be done in both directions since the legs will not contribute evenly to a lateral jump.

Lateral Jumps

Lateral Jump Single-Leg Landing

This drill is identical to the lateral jump but the landing is on one leg, the jump side leg. Single-leg lateral landings can place a lot of stress on the ankle and lateral knee ligaments of the landing leg if the weight of the upper body is not controlled, i.e., kept over the leg during the landing. This drill should be done on a firm, shock-absorbing surface like grass or a sprung wood floor, often found in fitness clubs. Sand and wrestling mats will increase the risk of injury by allowing the ankle to roll.

Lateral Box Jumps

Lateral Box Jump

This drill is a combination of the box jump and lateral jump. Stand an arm's length on the side of a box 24-40 inches high with feet hip width apart dip rapidly and explode upwards and sideways jumping onto the box. Be sure to land with both feet on the box at the same time. During the jump the knees will be pulled towards the chest to allow you to jump onto a higher box.

Multidirectional (Octagon) Hops

This is a combination plyometric and reaction drill, requiring the performer to react to a coach's command by jumping in the appropriate direction. Tape an octagonal pattern on the gym floor.

Label the sides 1 through 8 and place a 0 in the center of the pattern. Starting in the center, jump to the number called out by the coach or training partner and jump back to the center as quickly as possible. Perform 6-8 jumps per set, including two forward, two lateral and two backward jumps.

Rope Hops

This is an excellent drill for anyone involved in alpine skiing, particularly slalom events. Tie a rope between two supports approximately 12 inches off the ground. Stand facing along the rope with the side of your leg about 4 inches from the rope, feet close together. Hop sideways over the rope and back as quickly as possible driving off both feet and keeping them close together. Drive your arms upwards to help with the jump and to aid your balance. The hops can be directly side to side or you can increase the difficulty of the drill by jumping slightly diagonally and traveling along the rope as you hop. This drill is usually timed, with your objective being the completion of as many jumps as possible in a given time period.

Rope Jumps

Rope jumps are an advanced version of the rope hop. While the rope hop focuses on speed, the rope jump is designed to improve jump height and power. Tie a rope, angling the rope so that one end is 18 inches above the ground and the other is about 30 inches high. The rope should be at least 10 feet long to make the increase in height gradual enough to accommodate several jumps. Stand along the rope with the side of your leg about 4 inches from the rope, feet close together. Jump sideways over the rope and back, driving the arms upwards and pulling your knees toward your chest. Step forward a half step and jump again. Repeat this pattern until you either reach the end of the rope or cannot clear the height. A more difficult alternative is to jump slightly diagonally as you cross the rope, traveling the length of the rope.

Zig Zag Jump

With both feet together, hop diagonally as far as you can. As soon as you land, hop diagonally in the opposite direction following the pattern in the adjacent figure. Continue this pattern for 4-6 jumps.

Single Leg Jumps

Split Jump

Stand with feet shoulder width apart. Step forward into a lunge position. Keep your trunk upright. Jump upward as high as possible, pushing off of both legs and driving your arms upwards. Land in the same split position and take off again. When stepping forward into the lunge position remember to step straight forward, maintaining a shoulder width stance. It is common to bring the feet together when stepping forward, decreasing the

Split Jump

Scissor Jump

width of your base of support, making balance more difficult. An alternative is to switch legs in the air, landing with the opposite leg forward. If you do decide to switch legs, keep focusing on jumping as high as possible and not just on switching legs as fast as possible.

Scissor Jump

Set up as you did for the split jump. Place your feet shoulder width apart and take a long step forward into a lunge position. Jump as high as possible while driving the arms upward. While in the air scissor your legs by switching lead legs and switching them back so that you land in the original split position. The legs will have to be swung very quickly because the jump won't be very high from this position.

Single-Leg Hop

This is an introductory drill that everyone should use to get used to the technique, body position and balance needed for single-leg drills. Stand on one leg with the other leg bent behind at 90°, hands at your sides, looking straight ahead. Dip until your leg bends to 120° swinging the arms backwards as you dip. Swing the arms forward and up and hop upwards, focusing on completely extending the body, right through the calf. Land on the same leg you jumped from. Don't swing the back leg to try to increase jump height. Land and absorb the hop. Upon landing make sure the knee is solidly in line with the toe not wavering to either side. Your trunk should bend slightly but not more than 30°. If you cannot control the knee or trunk on landing you are not yet ready for single-leg drills, and need to improve leg and hip strength.

Single Leg Lateral Hop

Single-Leg Lateral Hop

This drill is performed exactly like the single-leg hop, only the hop is directly to the side rather than upward. Again, body control is essential, keeping the knee lined up with the foot and the trunk under control. You should be able to stick the landing without resorting to a secondary small hop to catch your balance. As you become accustomed to this drill, you can turn it into a multiple response drill by hopping laterally and back.

Single-Leg Tuck Jump

Stand on one leg with the other leg bent behind at 90°, hands at your sides, looking straight ahead. Dip until your leg bends to 120°, swinging the arms backwards as you dip. Drive the arms forward and up and explosively jump upwards as high as possible, focusing on completely extending the body. As you near the top of the jump, quickly bring the knee of the jump leg up to your chest. Land on the jump leg. Initially it may be necessary to land on the opposite leg until jump height or leg speed increases enough to allow you to land on the jump leg.

Single Leg Tuck Jump

Single-Leg Long Jump

This drill should be done into a sand pit or other very soft landing area. Stand on one leg with the other leg bent behind at 90°, hands at your sides, looking straight ahead. Dip until your leg bends to 120° swinging the arms backwards as you dip.

Drive the arms forward and up and explosively jump forward as far as possible. Swing both legs forward and land in the pit with both feet. A two foot landing is used to increase jump distance and protect the knees from unnecessary torque that may occur when landing in the sand. The difficulty of the exercise can be increased by not swinging the arms.

Single Leg Vertical Jump

Stand on one leg with the other leg bent behind at 90°, hands at your sides, looking straight ahead. Dip until your leg bends to 120°, swinging the arms backwards as you dip. Drive the arms forward and up and explosively jump upward as high as possible, focusing on completely extending the body.

Land on the same leg you jumped from. Don't swing the back leg to try to increase your jump. To increase the difficulty, perform this jump without swinging the arms. To further increase the difficulty this jump can be done as a multiple response jump where you jump again as soon as you land.

Single Leg Box Jump

This drill requires a box or set of boxes, varying in height from 15-45cm. The boxes should be solidly built with a non-slip landing surface. Stand on one leg facing the box

Single Leg Box Jump

with feet hip width to shoulder width apart, about an arm's length away from the box. Dip rapidly, swing the arms driving them upward and jump onto the box. Jump just high enough to land on the box in a half squat position. Return to the ground by stepping down or hopping off the box. Repeat with the other leg.

Push Off

Stand facing a box and place one foot completely on the box, the other foot remains on the ground. When the foot is on the box, the lower leg should be perpendicular to the ground and the thigh parallel to the floor creating a 90° angle at the knee. Lower boxes are also acceptable when first performing this drill.

Swing both arms upward as explosively as possible and push off against the box, jumping as high as possible, completely extending your body, reaching upward as high as possible. Land with the same foot on the box, the back foot should touch the ground just before the front leg absorbs the landing. This can be done as either a single or multiple response jump.

Push Off

Alternate Leg Push Off

Alternate Leg Push Off

Stand facing a box and place one foot completely on the box, the other foot remains on the ground. When the foot is on the box, the lower leg should be perpendicular to the ground and the thigh parallel to the floor creating a 90° angle at the knee. Lower boxes are acceptable when first performing this drill. Swing both arms upward as explosively as possible and push off against the box, jumping as high as possible, completely extending your body, reaching upward as high as possible. Switch feet in the air landing with the opposite foot on the box. This can be done as either a single or multiple response jump.

Lateral Push Off

Stand beside a box and place one foot completely on the box, the other foot remains on the ground. When the foot is on the box, the lower leg should be perpendicular to the ground and the thigh parallel to the floor creating a 90° angle at the knee. Swing both arms upward as explosively as possible and push off against the box, jumping as high as possible, completely extending your body, reaching upward as high as possible. Land with the same foot on the box, the back foot should touch the ground just before the front leg absorbs the landing. Increase the difficulty by using a higher box. This can be done as either a single or multiple response jump.

Lateral Push Off

Single Leg Lateral Jumps

Stand on one leg with the other leg bent behind at 90°, hands at your sides, looking straight ahead. Dip until your leg bends to 120°, swinging the arms backwards as you dip. Drive the arms forward and up and explosively jump sideways as far as possible, focusing on completely extending the body. Land on the same leg you jumped from. Perform jumps in both directions using the same leg before switching legs.

Alternate Leg Lateral Jumps

This is an excellent drill for athletes in skating sports. Stand on one leg with the other leg bent behind at 90°, hands at your sides, looking straight ahead. Dip until your leg bends to 120°, swinging the arms backwards as you dip.

Drive the arms forward and sideways, explosively jumping sideways as far as possible, focusing on completely extending the body. Drive the opposite leg out to the side to increase jump distance and prepare for landing. Land on the opposite leg and immediately jump back to the other side. Angled boxes can be made to improve the transfer of force and decrease the lateral stress on the knees.

Alternate Leg Lateral Jump

Diagonal Jump

Diagonal Jump

Stand on one leg with the other leg bent behind at 90°, hands at your sides, looking straight ahead. Dip until your leg bends to 120°, swinging the arms backwards as you dip. Drive the arms forward and toward your landing area, explosively jumping diagonally as far as possible, focusing on completely extending the body. Land on the same leg you jumped from. Perform jumps in both directions using the same leg before switching legs.

Alternate Leg Diagonal Jump

Stand on one leg with the other leg bent behind at 90°, hands at your sides, looking straight ahead. Dip until your leg bends to 120° swinging the arms backwards as you dip. Drive the arms forward and toward your landing area, explosively jumping diagonally as far as possible, focusing on completely extending the body. Swing the opposite leg toward the landing spot and land on the opposite foot.

Alternate Leg Diagonal Jump

CHAPTER 8

TRUNK PLYOMETRICS EXERCISES

V-Up

V-Up

Lie flat on your back, legs straight, hands extended overhead. Simultaneously bring your legs and trunk together, rising into a seated V position with legs in the air and trunk inclined. Hold this position for a two count and return to the ground, coming back up as soon as you touch the ground. Initially this drill will be done slowly until the balance point for your body is established. The drill should then become quicker and more explosive. This is an excellent drill for gymnasts and divers.

Seated Trunk Rotation

Sit in a V-up position, holding a medicine ball with both hands at arm's length in front of your chest. Keeping your arms straight, rotate from the trunk, turning as far as you can while maintaining the v-up position.

Seated Trunk Rotation

Quickly rotate back to the other side. There is a tendency to let the shoulders move during this exercise. Be sure to keep the ball high, moving only from the waist, following the ball with your head and shoulders, so that the ball stays in line with the mid point of your chest throughout the drill.

Leg Throws

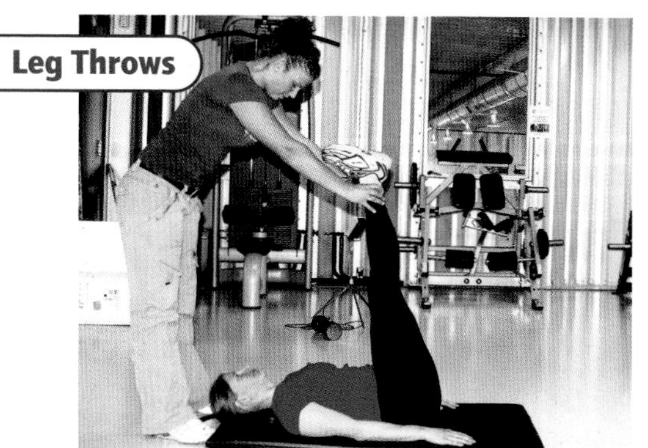

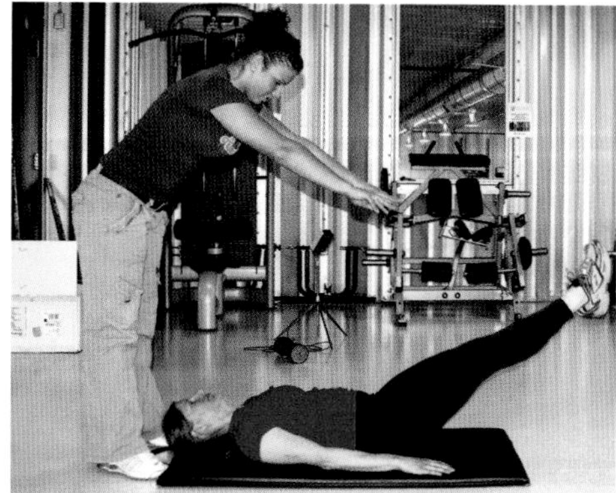

Leg Throws

Lie on the ground on your back, legs straight, holding onto your partner's ankles. Raise your legs so that they are perpendicular to the ground. Your partner will push your feet toward the floor. Just before your feet hit the ground stop the downward movement and explosively raise your legs again. The partner throwing the legs down should adjust the force so that the feet can be stopped without hitting the ground. With very strong athletes this drill can be done using a bench, allowing the thrower to stand to the side, where he will have better leverage for the throw. In either case, it is essential that the lower back remain in contact with the ground throughout this drill. Keep the abs contracted to accomplish this.

Sit Up Toss

Lie on your back with knees bent and feet flat on the floor. Come to the top sit up position and raise your hands overhead. Have a partner toss a medicine ball to your outstretched hands, allowing the weight to take you back to the bottom of the sit up. As soon as your shoulder blades touch the ground, explode upward and toss the ball back to your partner. The power for the throw should be generated predominantly from the abdominal muscles with the arms only coming into play for the final toss. The

Sit Up Toss

partner standing must make good, consistent throws into your hands so that a rhythm can be established. Don't raise your hips off the ground during the sit up. Instead, curl yourself up through the whole range of motion. If this drill is performed without the feet held down, the abdominal muscles will do most of the work. If the feet are held, the hip flexors will do most of the work.

Twisting Sit Up Toss

Lie on your back with knees bent and feet flat on the floor. Come to the top sit up position and raise your hands overhead. Have a partner toss a medicine ball to one side of your body at the level of your outstretched hands so that you have to rotate your trunk to catch the ball. Allow the weight to take you back to the bottom of the sit up without straightening your trunk. As soon as your shoulder blades touch the ground, sit up, maintaining the twist in your trunk, and throw the ball back to you partner. The power for the throw should be generated predominantly from the abdominal muscles with the arms only coming into play for the final toss. The partner standing must make good, consistent throws into your hands so that a rhythm can be established. Don't raise your hips off the ground during the sit up. Instead, curl yourself up through the whole range of motion. If this drill is performed without the feet held down, the abdominal muscles will do most of the work. If the feet are held, the hip flexors will do most of the work.

Twisting Sit Up Toss

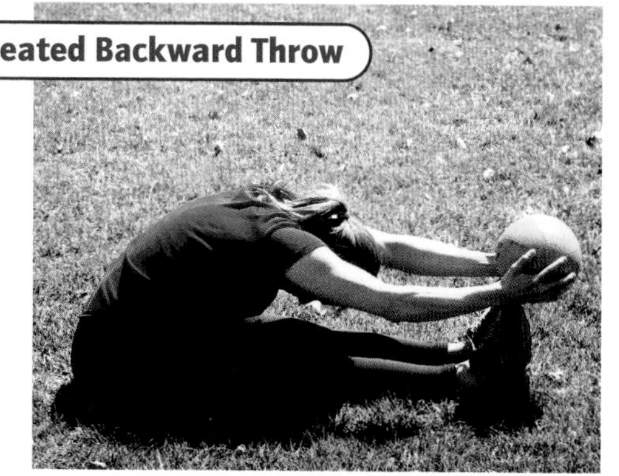

Seated Backward Throw

Seated Backward Throw

Sit on the floor or on a chair. Hold the medicine ball at arm's length overhead. Bend forward from the hips until your stomach touches your thighs, keeping the ball overhead. Maintain a straight back by sticking your chest out and pulling your shoulders back. This will keep your back in a strong, safe position and improve the distance you can throw. Explosively straighten your trunk and toss the ball as far backward as possible. The power for the throw comes from the trunk not the arms. Arm movement should be minimal so focus on keeping the muscles around the shoulders contracted. Arm strength will probably limit the weight of the ball that can be used. Choose a ball that you can throw with straight arms.

Pullover Toss

Lie on your back across a stability ball. Hips are low and the shoulders and back are supported by the ball. Hold a medicine ball at arm's length over your face. With elbows slightly bent, lower the medicine ball behind your head as far as possible. Quickly sit halfway up and toss the ball to your partner. Your partner will catch the ball and toss it back to your hands, which will remain overhead. Attention must be paid to making good throws so that a rhythm can be established.

Pullover Toss

Hanging Leg Toss

Hang from a pull up bar, arms and legs straight, holding a medicine ball between your feet, knees slightly bent. Without swinging your upper body, throw the ball forward as far as possible by bringing your feet explosively upward. Keep your abs tight throughout this drill. You will need a partner to return the ball to you. Weightlifting straps can improve your ability to hold on to the bar if this becomes the limiting factor in your ability to perform this drill.

Twist Toss

Stand sideways about 10 feet from your partner. Hold the medicine ball in both hands at waist height. Twist downward, pivoting on your feet and rotating at the trunk and hips. Quickly rotate in the opposite direction, driving through with your hips and coming onto your toes, in a movement similar to what you would use batting a baseball or hitting a golf ball. Keeping arms straight, throw the ball to your partner. The power for this throw comes from the pivot on the toes and firing of the hips around, it does not come from a rotation at the waist.

Twist Toss

Med. Ball High/Low Pass

Medicine Ball High/Low Pass

Stand back to back with a partner, 12-18 inches apart, feet slightly wider than shoulder width apart. Hold a medicine ball with both hands at arm's length in front of you. Raise the ball overhead with straight arms, bending backwards slightly and hand the ball to your partner, who is also reaching back. He will take the ball and bend over, passing it to you between his legs. Reach back up and pass the ball to him overhead. After 4-6 passes, reverse direction so that you pass the ball between your legs and he passes it overhead. Work to establish quick exchanges, always passing the ball with straight arms, letting your trunk do the work of moving the ball.

Medicine Ball Half Twist

Stand back to back with a partner, 6-12 inches apart, feet slightly wider than shoulder width apart. Hold a medicine ball with both hands at arm's length in front of you. Turn to your left and pass the ball to your partner, then turn back.

Med. Ball Half Twist

Medicine Ball Full Twist

Stand back to back with a partner, 6-12 inches apart, feet slightly wider than shoulder width apart, knees slightly bent. Hold a medicine ball with both hands at arm's length in front of you. Turn to your left and keeping your arms straight, pass the ball to your partner. Quickly turn to your right and receive the pass from him, turning all the way to your left to pass it again. After 4-6 passes, reverse directions.

High/Low Twisting Pass

Stand back to back with a partner, 12-18 inches apart, feet slightly wider than shoulder width apart. Hold a medicine ball with both hands at arm's length in front of you. Raise the ball overhead with straight arms, bending backwards slightly and to the side hand the ball to your partner, who is also reaching back and to the side. He will take the ball and bring it to waist height, twisting to the opposite side and passing it to you.

You will then bend from the hips, twist to the opposite side and pass the ball back to your partner at knee level. He will then stand up with the ball and rotate to the opposite side passing the ball overhead to you. Work to establish quick, smooth exchanges, always passing the ball with straight arms, letting your trunk do the work of moving the ball.

High/Low Twisting Pass

Straight Arm Standing Toss for Height

Stand with feet shoulder width apart, legs loose but not bent, weight distributed evenly on your feet. Holding a medicine ball straight in front of you, bend forward from the hips, sticking your rear end out and keeping your legs straight until the ball nearly touches the ground.

Explosively straighten your trunk out, coming back to an upright position. Keeping the arms straight, toss the ball as high as possible. Be sure to bend from the hips rather than bending from the waist. Bending from the hips allows you to keep your back flat and in a strong position to make the throw with minimal risk of injury.

Straight Arm Standing Toss for Height

Straight Arm Backward Overhead Toss

Stand with feet slightly wider than shoulder width apart, legs loose but not bent, weight distributed evenly on your feet. Holding a medicine ball straight overhead, bend forward from the hips, sticking your rear end out and keeping your legs straight until the ball nearly touches the ground.

Keeping your back flat by sticking your chest out and pulling your shoulders back, explosively straighten your trunk out, coming back to an upright position. Keeping the arms straight, toss the ball as far behind you as possible.

Straight Arm Backward Overhead Toss

FIU
VISITOR
PERIOD
FLORIDA INTERNATIONAL UNIVERSITY

CHAPTER 9

FULL BODY PLYOMETRICS

Underhand Toss for Height

Stand with feet slightly wider than shoulder width apart, holding a medicine ball at arm's length in front of you with both hands. Rapidly squat down to a quarter squat position, reversing direction as the ball gets below your knees. Jump explosively upward, driving with the legs and completely extending the trunk while accelerating the arms and ball upward to toss the ball as high as possible.

The majority of the power, and ball height comes from the jump, which must be as high as possible. The full body nature of this exercise will allow you to use a relatively heavy medicine ball, 10-30 lbs. Lighter balls can be used but require higher ceilings, if done indoors, and more space since the ball will be harder to control and have a tendency to travel, potentially falling on people doing drills nearby.

Single Arm Underhand Toss for Height

Single Arm Underhand Toss for Height

A throwing weight, kettle bell, or power ball is needed for this drill. Start in a quarter squat position with the implement in one hand, hanging between your feet just below knee height. Brace the opposite hand on your knee and slowly start swinging the weight between your legs.

On the third swing explode upward, extending the knees, hips, trunk and ankles while swinging the arm upward as explosively as possible. Throw the implement as high as possible. The upward leg drive and arm action should carry you off the ground. Repeat with the other arm.

Backward Underhand Toss

Set up exactly as you would for the underhand toss for height. Rapidly squat down to a quarter squat position, reversing direction as the ball gets below your knees. Jump explosively upward and backwards, driving with the legs and completely extending the trunk while accelerating the arms and ball upward to toss the ball as far as possible behind you.

Your momentum should carry you backwards and you will need to take a short hop or step to catch yourself. If this drill were done near a high jump landing mat, you could focus more of your power into a backward jump and land safely on the mat.

It will take some time and practice to find the optimal release point and timing for this drill. Avoid rapidly flexing the arms as you release the ball as this will cause a low trajectory and limit your throwing distance. Again, the majority of the power comes from the explosive jumping action, not the arms.

Backward Underhand Toss

Long Jump Toss

This drill is a combination of the underhand toss and a standing long jump. Stand with feet about shoulder width apart, holding a medicine ball in front of you at arm's length. Quickly dip until the knees bend to about 120 degrees. Explode forward extending the knees, hips, ankles and trunk while swinging the arms forward and upward as explosively as possible.

Toss the ball forward while jumping as far as possible. Focus on completely extending the body, reaching as high as possible. Swing the legs forward and land heels first, absorbing the impact with your legs, to maximize jumping distance. Practice with different release points until you find the one that gives you the farthest throw.

Timing is critical; the ball must be thrown just before your feet come off the ground so that you have a solid base from which to initiate the throw. If you throw late, while in the air, both throwing and jumping distance will be short.

Long Jump Toss

Forward Chest Pass

Forward Chest Pass

This drill is a combination of the standing long jump and chest pass. Stand with feet shoulder width apart, hold a medicine ball in front of you at arm's length, keeping your arms parallel to the ground. Quickly dip down until the knees bend to about 120 degrees and rapidly bend at the elbows, bringing the ball toward your chest. When the ball is 3-4 inches away from your chest, quickly reverse direction and push the ball away from yourself while jumping forward as far as possible.

Focus on completely extending the body and arms, reaching as far forward as possible. Swing the legs forward and land heels first, absorbing the impact with your legs, to maximize jumping distance. Keep your hands on the sides of the ball so that there is an even push with both arms. Again, timing is critical; the ball must be thrown just before the feet lose contact with the ground.

Repeat Underhand Toss for Height

Stand with feet slightly wider than shoulder width apart, holding a medicine ball at arm's length in front of you with both hands. Rapidly squat down to a quarter squat position, reversing direction as the ball gets below your knees. Jump explosively upward, driving with the legs and completely extending the trunk while accelerating the arms and ball upward to toss the ball as high as possible. Catch the ball in front of you with straight arms and allow it to bring you back into the quarter squat. Explode upward again, throwing the ball as high as possible. Repeat for as many reps as required. A very heavy medicine ball, 20lbs or more is needed for this drill so the ball cannot be thrown very high. High tosses break up the rhythm of the drill, turning it into a series of single throws rather than repeated tosses. Ideally, the ball should be heavy enough that the ball can only be thrown 12-15 feet high.

Side Lateral Toss

Side Lateral Toss

Stand with feet shoulder width apart, holding a handled medicine ball with one hand at waist height, elbow slightly bent. Without bending the trunk, move your arm to the side as explosively as possible and toss the ball sideways as far as you can. The release point for the ball will be just before the arm reaches shoulder level.

Bent Lateral Toss

Stand with feet shoulder width apart, holding a Power Grip Ball with one hand. Bend forward from the waist so that your trunk is parallel to the ground, elbow slightly bent. Move your arm to the side as explosively as possible and toss the ball sideways as far as you can. The release point for the ball will be just before the arm reaches shoulder level.

Bent Lateral Toss

Rotational Swings

Hold the Power Grip Ball at waist height with both hands, arms straight. Swing the ball in a circle similar to the action used in the first rotation of the hammer throw. The feet should stay still with all rotation coming from the upper body and trunk.

Spinning Throw

This drill is similar to the movement used in throwing a discuss. The ball will travel a long distance so an open field or catching net will be needed to keep those around you safe from injury.

Start facing away from the direction you intend to throw, feet shoulder width apart Power Grip Ball held in one hand. Step with your left foot so that it rotates around and is pointing in the opposite direction to where it started, bring your right leg around and repeat for another half rotation, releasing the ball when you are facing the opposite direction to where you started. Try to increase your speed with each rotation.

Standing Side Arm Throw

Standing Side Arm Throw

Stand with feet shoulder width apart, holding a Power Grip Ball in your right hand, left foot slightly ahead of your right foot. Rotate your body clockwise and down, corkscrewing yourself towards the ground, turning on your toes so that your whole body and not just your trunk turns. Keeping your arm straight, fire your hips around and up throwing the ball as far as possible. The power for this drill is developed through the hips and trunk. The drill should be repeated on the left side.

Overhead Tricep Toss

Hold a Power Grip Ball in one hand, arm straight overhead. Bend your arm so that your elbow is perpendicular to the ground, pointing straight upward.

The ball should be just behind your head. Straighten your arm as quickly as possible and toss the ball into the air using only your triceps.

Overhead Tricep Toss

POWER
SYSTEMS

CHAPTER 10

LEVEL 1 PROGRAM

The Level 1 program is for those people who score above 40 on the movement screening described in Chapter 3. Level 1 people exhibit an inability to control their bodies, increasing their risk of injury when performing high intensity speed and power activities. The Level 1 program is an eight-week program designed to address body control and basic movement technique. Typically, only 15-20% of people will fall into Level 1. Those who do, need to be monitored closely and pay particular attention to the technique of every exercise performed.

The reasons for scoring in Level 1 are very individual, but three common groups have emerged from the analysis of the testing that was done when the movement screening was created. Some people have true weaknesses or muscle imbalances that may be the result of past injury, the unilateral nature of their sport or improper training. Depending on their severity, muscle weaknesses and imbalances can take a while to correct. These people should repeat the movement screening every four weeks to measure progress.

Others are new to sport or are returning to sport after being away for many years. These people are inexperienced at athletic movement and body control. Very often they have been involved in desk jobs with low physical demands, and their physical activity has been limited to machine-based strength training and unidirectional aerobic conditioning. For these people, moving from Level 1 to Level 2 often occurs quite quickly as they learn basic movement skills and techniques. These people should repeat the movement screening every two weeks for the eight weeks of the program.

The third common group that has emerged is comprised of teens and pre-teens going through their major growth spurts. During periods of rapid growth, it is quite common to see decreases in flexibility, movement skill and strength to weight ratios as the young athlete adjusts to the dramatic changes in his body. Performance often returns quickly as the athlete learns to control the longer, larger limbs and flexibility returns as the length of the muscles catches up to the length of the bones. Progress from Level 1 to Level 2 can be quite quick as the athletes' bodies are capable of adapting very rapidly at this point in their development. The movement screening should be repeated monthly until they move to Level 2.

Using the Program

The program is eight weeks long and progresses from the simplest to the most complex Level 1 drills and exercises. Each workout is designed to last 60 minutes and can be done with a group or individually. The workouts are broken into five sections; warm-up, balance training, strength training, speed and agility, and cool down stretching. Within each section, the exercises are to be done as a circuit, meaning the athlete is to perform an exercise and then immediately move on to the next station, taking only the time needed to change exercises as a rest. This style of circuit training creates a situation similar to a random practice used in skill teaching. Random practice has been shown to enhance long-term learning and improve the athlete's ability to adapt to new skills and physical challenges.

The workouts are to be performed three times per week, with at least 48 hours between sessions. Other strength and conditioning workouts should be avoided at this time as the athlete is not physically capable of performing them effectively.

If an athlete has not progressed to Level 2 by the end of the eight-week program, repeat the final two weeks one more time. If he still has not moved up to Level 2, have a medical doctor or physical therapist perform an orthopedic evaluation to determine if there are any underlying problems that need to be corrected.

Descriptions of the exercises that are not self-explanatory are included in Chapter 5.

Level 1 Week 1 and 2

Warm-up (5 minutes)

- 30s forward jogging
- 30s backward jogging
- 30s lateral jogging clockwise
- 30s lateral jogging counterclockwise
- 15s arm swings
- 10 alternate toe touches
- 10 walking high kicks

Balance Training (15 minutes)

Take two minutes to orient the group or yourself to what they will be doing at each station. If you are dealing with a larger group, break the group into five smaller groups of no more than five athletes. Each group will spend 60 seconds at a station before moving in a clockwise direction to the next station. Complete the whole circuit twice before moving onto the next part of the workout.

Station 1: Single leg T balance
Station 2: Eyes closed single leg balance
Station 3: Swiss ball partner perturbations

Station 4: Single leg tennis ball toss – change legs every five throws
Station 5: Single leg medicine ball pick ups

Strength (15 minutes)

Take two minutes to orient the group to what they will be doing at each station. Break the large group into five smaller groups of no more than five athletes. Each group will spend 120 seconds at each station before moving in a clockwise direction to the next station. Complete the whole circuit three times before moving onto the next part of the workout.

Station 1: Walking lunges – 10 reps
Station 2: Medicine ball chest pass – 10 passes
Station 3: Lateral lunges – 10 reps
Station 4: Inch worms – 10m
Station 5: Step ups – 30cm plyobox – 10 reps each leg

Water Break (5 minutes)

Agility, Quickness and Speed (15 minutes)

Take two minutes to orient the group to what they will be doing at each station. Break the large group into five smaller groups of no more than five athletes. Each group will spend 60 seconds at each station before moving in a clockwise direction to the next station. Complete the whole circuit twice before moving onto the next part of the workout. If you are doing this workout alone, take a 30s rest after each repeat of the drill.

Station 1: 10m box drill with rounding the corner – clockwise the first time through, counterclockwise the second – repeat three times each direction.
Station 2: Lateral high knee hurdles – 6 x 15cm step hurdles – alternate lead legs – repeat three times
Station 3: Forward high knee hurdles – 30cm step hurdles
Station 4: Back pedal/sprint forward – 15m each direction
Station 5: Carioca* – 15m each direction

Cool Down (5 minutes)

- Calf stretch
- Hurdler's stretch
- Groin stretch
- Hip stretch
- Shoulder stretch

Hold each stretch for 3 sets of 15 seconds.

* shoulders square, bring feet together and move laterally using a cross-over step for the recommended distance

Level 1 Week 3 and 4

Warm-up (5 minutes)

- 30s High knee forward jogging
- 30s backward jogging
- 30s lateral shuffle
- 30s Carioca jogging
- 15s arm swings
- 10 alternate toe touches
- 10 walking high kicks

Balance (15 minutes)

Take two minutes to orient the group to what they will be doing at each station. Break the large group into five smaller groups of no more than five athletes. Each group will spend 60 seconds at each station before moving in a clockwise direction to the next station. Complete the whole circuit twice before moving onto the next part of the workout.

Station 1: Swiss ball seated balance
Station 2: Eyes closed single leg balance
Station 3: Swiss ball partner perturbations
Station 4: Skating position single leg tennis ball toss – change legs every five throws
Station 5: Single leg medicine ball pick ups

Strength (15 minutes)

Take two minutes to orient the group to what they will be doing at each station. Break the large group into five smaller groups of no more than five athletes. Each group will spend 120 seconds at each station before moving in a clockwise direction to the next station. Complete the whole circuit three times before moving onto the next part of the workout.

Station 1: Medicine ball squats – 10 reps
Station 2: Medicine ball toss for height – 10 passes
Station 3: Clock lunges – six points on the clock with each leg
Station 4: Inch worms – 10m
Station 5: Crossover step ups – 30cm box – 10 reps each leg

Water Break (5 minutes)

Agility, Quickness and Speed (15 minutes)

Take two minutes to orient the group to what they will be doing at each station. Break the large group into five smaller groups of no more than five athletes. Each group will spend 60 seconds at each station before moving in a clockwise direction to the next station. Complete the whole circuit twice before moving onto the next part of the workout. If you are doing the workout alone, take a 30s rest between repeats of each drill.

Station 1: 10m box drill with rounding the corner – clockwise the first time through, counterclockwise the second – repeat three times each direction.

Station 2: Lateral high knee hurdles – 6 x15cm step hurdles – alternate lead legs repeat three times

Station 3: Forward high knee hurdles – 6 x 30cm step hurdles – repeat three times

Station 4: Back pedal/sprint forward – 15m each direction – repeat three times

Station 5: Carioca – 15m each direction – repeat three times

Cool Down (5 minutes)

- Calf stretch
- Hurdler's stretch
- Groin stretch
- Hip stretch
- Shoulder stretch

Hold each stretch for 3 sets of 15 seconds.

Level 1 Week 5 and 6

Warm-up (5 minutes)

- 30s Butt kick jogging
- 30s backward jogging
- 30s Walking B's
- 30s Carioca jogging
- 15s arm swings
- 10 alternate toe touches
- 10 walking high kicks

Balance (15 minutes)

Take two minutes to orient the group to what they will be doing at each station. Break the large group into five smaller groups of no more than five athletes. Each group will spend 60 seconds at each station before moving in a clockwise direction to the next station. Complete the whole circuit twice before moving onto the next part of the workout.

Station 1: Swiss ball seated balance
Station 2: Box Landings
Station 3: Swiss ball partner perturbations
Station 4: Skating position single leg tennis ball toss – change legs every five throws
Station 5: Board stepping

Strength (15 minutes)

Take two minutes to orient the group to what they will be doing at each station. Break the large group into five smaller groups of no more than five athletes. Each group will spend 120 seconds at each station before moving in a clockwise direction to the next station. Complete the whole circuit three times before moving onto the next part of the workout.

Station 1: Medicine ball squats – 3 x 10 reps
Station 2: Tubing overhead press – 3 x 10
Station 3: Clock lunges – 3 x clock
Station 4: Medicine ball chest pass – 3 x 10
Station 5: Crossover step ups – 30cm box – 3 x 10 reps

Water Break (5 minutes)

Agility, Quickness and Speed (15 minutes)

Take two minutes to orient the group to what they will be doing at each station. Break the large group into five smaller groups of no more than five athletes. Each group will spend 60 seconds at each station before moving in a clockwise direction to the next station. Complete the whole circuit twice before moving onto the next part of the workout. If you are doing the workout alone, take a 30s rest between repeats of each drill.

Station 1: 180o turn sprints – 15m – clockwise the first time through, counterclockwise the second – repeat three times

Station 2: Lateral high knee hurdles – 6 x 30cm step hurdles – alternate lead legs – repeat three times

Station 3: Ladder forward, backward and lateral run series – agility ladder – repeat two times

Station 4: Back pedal/sprint forward – 15m each direction – repeat three times

Station 5: Hurdle two foot hops – 6 x 15cm hurdles – repeat two times

Cool Down (5 minutes)

- Calf stretch
- Hurdler's stretch
- Groin stretch
- Hip stretch
- Shoulder stretch

Hold each stretch for 3 sets of 15 seconds.

Level 1 Week 7

Warm-up (5 minutes)

- 30s Butt kick jogging
- 30s backward jogging
- 30s Walking B's
- 30s Carioca jogging
- 15s arm swings
- 10 alternate toe touches
- 10 walking high kicks

Balance (15 minutes)

Take two minutes to orient the group to what they will be doing at each station. Break the large group into five smaller groups of no more than five athletes. Each group will spend 60 seconds at each station before moving in a clockwise direction to the next station. Complete the whole circuit twice before moving onto the next part of the workout.

Station 1: Swiss ball seated balance raise one leg
Station 2: Box landings
Station 3: Prone support
Station 4: Skating position single leg tennis ball toss – change legs every five throws
Station 5: Board stepping

Strength (15 minutes)

Take two minutes to orient the group to what they will be doing at each station. Break the large group into five smaller groups of no more than five athletes. Each group will spend 120 seconds at each station before moving in a clockwise direction to the next station. Complete the whole circuit three times before moving onto the next part of the workout.

Station 1: Medicine ball squats – 10 reps – 6lb med ball
Station 2: Tubing overhead press – 10 reps
Station 3: Clock lunges – 6 stops on the clock each leg
Station 4: Swiss ball walkouts – 5 walkouts
Station 5: Medicine ball over/under partner pass – 10 passes

Water Break (5 minutes)

Agility, Quickness and Speed (15 minutes)

Take two minutes to orient the group to what they will be doing at each station. Break the large group into five smaller groups of no more than five athletes. Each group will spend 60 seconds at each station before moving in a clockwise direction to the next station. Complete the whole circuit twice before moving onto the next part of the workout. If you are doing the workout alone, take a 30s rest between repeats of each drill.

Station 1: 180° turn sprints – 15m – clockwise the first time through counterclockwise the second – repeat three times

Station 2: Lateral high knee hurdles – 6 x 30cm step hurdles – alternate lead legs– repeat three times

Station 3: Ladder icky shuffle, buzz saws – agility ladder – repeat three times

Station 4: Lateral shuffle medicine ball pick up – 4lb med ball – 5m each direction – repeat three times

Station 5: Hurdle two-foot hops – 6 x 15cm hurdles – repeat two times

Cool Down (5 minutes)

- Calf stretch
- Hurdler's stretch
- Groin stretch
- Hip stretch
- Shoulder stretch

Hold each stretch for 3 sets of 15 seconds.

Level 1 Week 8

Warm-up (5 minutes)

- 30s Butt kick jogging
- 30s backward jogging
- 30s Walking B's
- 30s Carioca jogging
- 15s arm swings
- 10 alternate toe touches
- 10 walking high kicks

Balance (15 minutes)

Take two minutes to orient the group to what they will be doing at each station. Break the large group into five smaller groups of no more than five athletes. Each group will spend 60 seconds at each station before moving in a clockwise direction to the next station. Complete the whole circuit twice before moving onto the next part of the workout.

Station 1: Swiss ball kneeling balance
Station 2: Box landings lateral shuffle
Station 3: Supine leg raise
Station 4: Skating position single leg tennis ball toss – change legs every five throws
Station 5: Board stepping medicine ball toss

Strength (15 minutes)

Take two minutes to orient the group to what they will be doing at each station. Break the large group into five smaller groups of no more than five athletes. Each group will spend 120 seconds at each station before moving in a clockwise direction to the next station. Complete the whole circuit three times before moving onto the next part of the workout.

Station 1: Crossover step ups – 10 reps
Station 2: Sit up toss – 10 reps – 4lb med ball
Station 3: Tubing partner rows – 10 reps
Station 4: Swiss ball walkouts – 5 push ups – 3 reps
Station 5: Medicine ball rotational partner pass – 10 reps

Water Break (5 minutes)

Agility, Quickness and Speed (15 minutes)

Take two minutes to orient the group to what they will be doing at each station. Break the large group into five smaller groups of no more than five athletes. Each group will spend 60 seconds at each station before moving in a clockwise direction to the next station. Complete the whole circuit twice before moving onto the next part of the workout. If you are doing the workout alone, take a 30s rest between repeats of each drill.

Station 1: 180o turn sprints – 15 m – clockwise the first time through, counterclockwise the second – repeat three times

Station 2: Lateral high knee hurdles – 6 x 30cm step hurdles – alternate lead legs – repeat three times

Station 3: Ladder icky shuffle, buzz saws – agility ladder – repeat three times

Station 4: Lateral shuffle medicine ball pick up – 4lb med ball – 5m each direction – repeat three times

Station 5: Hurdle two-foot hops – 6 x 15cm hurdles – repeat two times

Cool Down (5 minutes)

- Calf stretch
- Hurdler's stretch
- Groin stretch
- Hip stretch
- Shoulder stretch

Hold each stretch for 3 sets of 15 seconds.

CHAPTER 11

LEVEL 2 PROGRAM

The Level 2 program is for those people who score between 22 and 39 on the movement screening described in Chapter 3. Level 2 people exhibit varying degrees of strength and flexibility imbalances that affect their ability to fully control their bodies during higher speed and higher intensity movements. The majority of people, about 60%, will receive scores that place them in Level 2 when first doing the movement screening test. Many people who were formerly Level 3 will test at Level 2 when returning from an injury. The time to progress form Level 2 to Level 3 varies considerably from person to person.

Using the Program

The program is eight weeks long and progresses from the simplest to the most complex Level 2 drills and exercises. The goal of the Level 2 program is to improve the athlete's ability to control his body in higher speed, higher intensity drills featuring rapid changes of direction. It is essential that good form is used for every repetition of every drill. Sloppy performance defeats the purpose of the program and will slow the athlete's ability to move to the next level of programming.

Each workout is designed to last 60 minutes and can be done with a group or individually. The workouts are broken into three sections; warm-up, speed, agility and power training, and cool down stretching. Within each section, the exercises are to be done as a circuit, meaning the athlete is to perform an exercise and then immediately move on to the next station, taking only the time needed to change exercises as a rest. This style of circuit training creates a situation similar to a random practice used in skill teaching. Random practice has been shown to enhance long-term learning and improve the athlete's ability to adapt to new skills and physical challenges.

The workouts are to be performed three times per week, with at least 48 hours between sessions. A full body strength training program should be undertaken 2-3 times per week in conjunction with the program outlined here. The strength program should emphasize core and hip strength through large multi-joint exercises like squats, dead lifts and leg presses.

If an athlete has not progressed to Level 3 by the end of the eight-week program, repeat the final two weeks one more time. If he still has not moved up to Level 2, have a medical doctor or physical therapist perform an orthopedic evaluation to determine if there are any underlying problems that need to be corrected.

Descriptions of the exercises that are not self-explanatory are included in Chapter 5.

Level 2 Week 1

Warm-up (5 minutes)

- 30s Butt kick jogging
- 30s backward jogging
- 30s Walking lunges
- 30s Carioca jogging
- 15s arm swings
- 10 alternate toe touches
- 10 walking high kicks

Agility, Quickness and Speed (45 minutes)

Take two minutes to orient the athletes to what they will be doing at each station. Break the large group into smaller groups of no more than five athletes. Each group will spend two minutes at each station before moving in a clockwise direction to the next station. Continue to work at the station for the full two minutes. If you are training alone, take a 20s break after each time through the station. Complete the whole circuit twice before moving onto the next part of the workout. Take a five-minute water break after the first circuit is completed.

Station 1: Power sled push and drag – add 45lbs of weight – 20m
Station 2: High knee lateral hurdles – 15 m step hurdles – two rows
Station 3: 15m sprint 90° cut – alternate cut left and right
Station 4: Medicine ball seated rotational throw – 4 and 6lb. balls – 8 reps
Station 5: Box drill – backpedal to lateral shuffle to forward sprint to lateral shuffle – 10m
Station 6: Box jumps – jump onto box, step off – 4x set of boxes
Station 7: Up and Back – 7.5 m
Station 8: Medicine ball toss for height – 8 and 10lb balls – 8 reps
Station 9: Inch worm – 10 m
Station 10: T-Drill

Cool Down (10 minutes)

- Calf stretch
- Hurdler's stretch
- Quad stretch
- Groin stretch
- Hip stretch
- Shoulder stretch

Hold each stretch for 3 sets of 20 seconds.

Level 2 Week 2

Warm-up (5 minutes)

- 30s Butt kick jogging
- 30s backward jogging
- 30s Walking lunges
- 30s Carioca jogging
- 15s arm swings
- 10 alternate toe touches
- 10 walking high kicks

Agility, Quickness and Speed (45 minutes)

Take two minutes to orient the athletes to what they will be doing at each station. Break the large group into smaller groups of no more than five athletes. Each group will spend two minutes at each station before moving in a clockwise direction to the next station. Continue to work at the station for the full two minutes. If you are training alone, take a 20s break after each time through the station. Complete the whole circuit twice before moving onto the next part of the workout. Take a five-minute water break after the first circuit is completed.

Station 1:	Power sled push and drag – add 45lbs of weight –15m
Station 2:	High knee forward hurdles – 30cm step hurdles- two rows
Station 3:	Medicine ball sit up toss – 4 and 6lb balls
Station 4:	Hurdle M-Drill – 15cm hurdles
Station 5:	Back pedal 90o cuts – alternate cut left and cut right
Station 6:	Box jumps – jump onto box, step off – 4x set of boxes
Station 7:	Lateral shuffles – 5m x 5
Station 8:	Medicine ball long jump toss - 8 and 10lb balls – 8 reps
Station 9:	Inch worm – 10 m
Station 10:	Star-Drill

Cool Down (10 minutes)

- Calf stretch
- Hurdler's stretch
- Quad stretch
- Groin stretch
- Hip stretch
- Shoulder stretch

Hold each stretch for 3 sets of 20 seconds.

Level 2 Week 3

Warm-up (5 minutes)

- 30s Butt kick jogging
- 30s backward jogging
- 30s Walking lunges
- 30s Carioca jogging
- 15s arm swings
- 10 alternate toe touches
- 10 walking high kicks

Agility, Quickness and Speed (45 minutes)

Take two minutes to orient the athletes to what they will be doing at each station. Break the large group into smaller groups of no more than five athletes. Each group will spend two minutes at each station before moving in a clockwise direction to the next station. Continue to work at the station for the full two minutes. If you are training alone, take a 20s break after each time through the station. Complete the whole circuit twice before moving onto the next part of the workout. Take a five minute water break after the first circuit is completed.

Station 1: Power sled push and drag – add 70lbs of weight – 15m
Station 2: High knee lateral hurdles backpedal – 30cm step hurdles – two rows
Station 3: Prone support – 30s holds rest 30s
Station 4: Backward hurdle hops – 15cm hurdles
Station 5: Partner resisted sprints – 10m
Station 6: Lateral Box jumps – jump onto box step off – 4x set of boxes
Station 7: Figure 8 Sprints – 10 m x 2
Station 8: Supine leg raises – 30s hold rest 30s
Station 9: Two person get up and react
Station 10: T-drill

Cool down (10 minutes)

- Calf stretch
- Hurdler's stretch
- Quad stretch
- Groin stretch
- Hip stretch
- Shoulder stretch

Hold each stretch for 3 sets of 20 seconds.

Level 2 Week 4

Warm-up (5 minutes)

- 30s Butt kick jogging
- 30s backward jogging
- 30s Walking lunges
- 30s Carioca jogging
- 15s arm swings
- 10 alternate toe touches
- 10 walking high kicks

Agility, Quickness and Speed (45 minutes)

Take two minutes to orient the athletes to what they will be doing at each station. Break the large group into smaller groups of no more than five athletes. Each group will spend two minutes at each station before moving in a clockwise direction to the next station. Continue to work at the station for the full two minutes. If you are training alone, take a 20s break after each time through the station. Complete the whole circuit twice before moving onto the next part of the workout. Take a five-minute water break after the first circuit is completed.

Station 1: Power sled push and drag – add 80lbs of weight – 15m
Station 2: Box drill sprint forward to lateral shuffle to back pedal to lateral shuffle, cuts at the corners – 5m per side
Station 3: Medicine ball sit up toss – 4 and 6lb. balls – 3 x 10 reps
Station 4: Backward hurdle hops – 15cm hurdles
Station 5: Partner resisted lateral shuffles – 10m
Station 6: Multiple box jumps – jump onto box hop off – 4x set of boxes
Station 7: Figure 8 sprints – 7.5 m x 4
Station 8: Med ball rotational toss – 4 and 6 lb balls
Station 9: Two person get up and react
Station 10: T-drill

Cool Down (10 minutes)

- Calf stretch
- Hurdler's stretch
- Quad stretch
- Groin stretch
- Hip stretch
- Shoulder stretch

Hold each stretch for 3 sets of 20 seconds.

Level 2 Week 5

Warm-up (5 minutes)

- 30s Butt kick jogging
- 30s backward jogging
- 30s Walking lunges
- 30s Carioca jogging
- 15s arm swings
- 10 alternate toe touches
- 10 walking high kicks

Agility, Quickness and Speed (45 minutes)

Take two minutes to orient the athletes to what they will be doing at each station. Break the large group into smaller groups of no more than five athletes. Each group will spend two minutes at each station before moving in a clockwise direction to the next station. Continue to work at the station for the full two minutes. If you are training alone, take a 20s break after each time through the station. Complete the whole circuit twice before moving onto the next part of the workout. Take a five-minute water break after the first circuit is completed.

Station 1:	Power sled push and drag – add 80 lbs of weight – 15m
Station 2:	Reaction belts – best of 5 – 15s per trial
Station 3:	Medicine ball long jump toss – 10 and 12 lb. balls – 3 x 5 reps
Station 4:	Backward hurdle hops – 15 cm hurdles
Station 5:	Partner resisted lateral shuffles – 10m
Station 6:	Multiple box jumps – jump onto box hop off – 4x set of boxes
Station 7:	Figure 8 sprints – 7.5 m x 4
Station 8:	Medicine ball rotational toss – 4 and 6 lb balls
Station 9:	Reaction ball grounders – groups of 2-3
Station 10:	T-drill

Cool Down (10 minutes)

- Calf Stretch
- Hurdler's stretch
- Quad stretch
- Groin stretch
- Hip stretch
- Shoulder stretch

Hold each stretch for 3 sets of 20 seconds.

Level 2 Week 6

Warm-up (5 minutes)

- 30s Butt kick jogging
- 30s backward jogging
- 30s Walking lunges
- 30s Carioca jogging
- 15s arm swings
- 10 alternate toe touches
- 10 walking high kicks

Agility, Quickness and Speed (45 minutes)

Take two minutes to orient the athletes to what they will be doing at each station. Break the large group into smaller groups of no more than five athletes. Each group will spend two minutes at each station before moving in a clockwise direction to the next station. Continue to work at the station for the full two minutes. If you are training alone, take a 20s break after each time through the station. Complete the whole circuit twice before moving onto the next part of the workout. Take a five-minute water break after the first circuit is completed.

Station 1: Power sled figure – 8 push and drag – add 90 lbs of weight – 15m
Station 2: Reaction belts – best of 5 – 15s per trial
Station 3: Medicine ball overhead pass – 4 and 6 lb balls – 3 x 5 reps
Station 4: Ladder icky shuffle, forward runs and buzz saws
Station 5: Star drill – go through patern twice, then switch
Station 6: Box speed jumps – on and off – 10 reps as fast as possible
Station 7: Back pedal figure – 8 – 5m
Station 8: Supine power drop – 8-10 lb med balls
Station 9: Reaction ball grounders – groups of 2-3
Station 10: High knee lateral hurdles – 30 cm hurdles

Cool Down (10 minutes)

- Calf Stretch
- Hurdler's stretch
- Quad stretch
- Groin stretch
- Hip stretch
- Shoulder stretch

Hold each stretch for 3 sets of 20 seconds.

Level 2 Week 7

Warm-up (5 minutes)

- 30s Butt kick jogging
- 30s backward jogging
- 30s Walking lunges
- 30s Carioca jogging
- 15s arm swings
- 10 alternate toe touches
- 10 walking high kicks

Agility, Quickness and Speed (25 minutes)

Take two minutes to orient the athletes to what they will be doing at each station. Break the large group into smaller groups of no more than five athletes. Each group will spend two minutes at each station before moving in a clockwise direction to the next station. Continue to work at the station for the full two minutes. If you are training alone, take a 20s break after each time through the station. Complete the whole circuit twice before moving onto the next part of the workout. Take a five-minute water break after the first circuit is completed.

Station 1: Power sled figure – 8 push and drag – add 120 lbs of weight – 15m

Station 2: Reaction ball grounders – groups of 2-3

Station 3: Medicine ball sit up toss – 4 and 6 lb balls – 3 x 5 reps

Station 4: Partner resisted lateral shuffles – 10m

Station 5: Box jump into high knee lateral hurdle – 30cm hurdles

Energy System Training (20 minutes)

Take two minutes to orient the athletes to what they will be doing at each station. Break the large group into smaller groups of no more than five athletes. Each group will spend four minutes at each station before moving in a clockwise direction to the next station. Continue to work at the station for the full two minutes. If you are training alone, take a 20s break after each time through the station. Complete the whole circuit twice before moving onto the next part of the workout. Take a five-minute water break after the first circuit is completed.

Station 1: Linear sprints – 50m

Station 2: Up and back – 20m

Station 3: Box drill – sprinting forward around cone, turn at every corner

Station 4: T-drill – do the pattern twice, then switch

Station 5: Star drill – do the patern twice, then switch

Cool Down (5 minutes)

- Calf stretch
- Hurdler's stretch
- Quad stretch
- Groin stretch
- Hip stretch
- Shoulder stretch

Hold each stretch for 2 sets of 20 seconds.

Level 2 Week 8

Warm-up (5 minutes)

- 30s Butt kick jogging
- 30s backward jogging
- 30s Walking lunges
- 30s Carioca jogging
- 15s arm swings
- 10 alternate toe touches
- 10 walking high kicks

Agility, Quickness and Speed (25 minutes)

Take two minutes to orient the athletes to what they will be doing at each station. Break the large group into smaller groups of no more than five athletes. Each group will spend two minutes at each station before moving in a clockwise direction to the next station. Continue to work at the station for the full two minutes.

If you are training alone take a 20s break after each time through the station. Complete the whole circuit twice before moving onto the next part of the workout. Take a five minute water break after the first circuit is completed.

Station 1: Power sled drag – add 120 lbs of weight – 15m

Station 2: Reaction belt – best of five- maximum 15s per trial

Station 3: Medicine ball rotational toss – 4 and 6 lb balls

Station 4: Partner resisted forward, and back pedal sprints – 10m

Station 5: Box jump into high knee lateral hurdle – 30cm hurdles

Energy System Training (20 minutes)

Take two minutes to orient the athletes to what they will be doing at each station. Break the large group into smaller groups of no more than five athletes. Each group will spend four minutes at each station before moving in a clockwise direction to the next station.

Continue to work at the station for the full two minutes. If you are training alone take a 20s break after each time through the station. Complete the whole circuit twice before moving onto the next part of the workout. Take a five minute water break after the first circuit is completed.

Station 1: Linear sprints – 50m

Station 2: Lateral shuffles – 10m between cones

Station 3: Back pedal box Drill – backpedal around every cone, round each corner

Station 4: M-drill – do the pattern twice, then switch

Station 5: Hurdle T-drill

Cool Down (5 minutes)

- Calf stretch
- Hurdler's stretch
- Quad stretch
- Groin stretch
- Hip stretch
- Shoulder stretch

Hold each stretch for 2 sets of 20 seconds.

CHAPTER 12

PLYO PROGRAMS

The programs in this chapter are to be used after you have achieved Level 3 on the movement screening outlined in Chapter 3. You should also have at least 12 months of formal strength training experience. For the purposes of this book, beginners will be considered those athletes with no prior plyometric training experience, intermediate are those with 1-2 years of experience and advanced are those athletes with more than 2 years of plyometrics training.

If you are an intermediate or advanced athlete, use the beginner program for 2-3 weeks before moving to the intermediate program. Advanced athletes will then use the intermediate program for two weeks before moving on to the advanced program. This builds some variety and progression into the program so that you do not increase your plyo volume too quickly and injure yourself.

Ice Hockey

The goal of the ice hockey plyometric program is to develop lower body and trunk power. The lower body emphasis is on single-leg lateral and diagonal movements similar to the motions used in the skating stride. The upper body emphasis is on rotational movements to build shot power. These programs are performed late in the pre season phase of training, 2 days per week, and should be complemented with strength training and sport-specific anaerobic conditioning.

Beginner		
Exercise	**Sets**	**Reps**
Standing long jump	3	5
Lateral hurdle hops	3	5
Multidirectional hops	2	5
Seated trunk rotation	3	8
Twisting sit up toss	4	5

Intermediate		
Exercise	**Sets**	**Reps**
Alternate leg diagonal jump	3	5
Single-leg hop	4	5
Lateral jump single-leg landing	3	5
Twist toss	3	5
Straight arm standing toss for height	3	5

Advanced		
Exercise	**Sets**	**Reps**
Single-leg lateral hop	3	5
Alternate leg push-off	4	5
Single-leg long jump	3	5
Alternate leg lateral jump	4	5
Rotational swings	4	5
Hanging leg toss	4	5

Baseball/Softball

The goal of the baseball/softball plyometric program is to develop lower body and trunk power. The lower body emphasis is on single-leg lateral and diagonal movements similar to the motions used in the running stride. The upper body emphasis is on rotational movements to develop swing and throwing. These programs are performed late in the pre-season phase of training, 2 days per week, and should be complemented with strength training and sport-specific anaerobic conditioning.

Beginner		
Exercise	**Sets**	**Reps**
Standing long jump	3	5
Lateral hurdle hops	3	5
Multidirectional hops	2	5
Seated trunk rotation	3	8
Twisting sit up toss	4	5

Intermediate		
Exercise	**Sets**	**Reps**
Alternate leg diagonal jump	3	5
Single lep hop	4	5
Lateral jump single-leg landing	3	5
Twist toss	3	5
Straight arm standing toss for height	3	5

Advanced		
Exercise	**Sets**	**Reps**
Single-leg lateral hop	3	5
Alternate leg push-off	4	5
Single-leg long jump	3	5
Alternate leg lateral jump	4	5
One arm heavy bag push	4	5
Side lateral toss	4	5

Football

The goal of the football plyometric program is to develop full body power to improve power off the line when the ball is snapped. These programs are performed late in the pre-season phase of training, 2 days per week, and should be complemented with strength training and sport-specific anaerobic conditioning.

Beginner		
Exercise	**Sets**	**Reps**
Tuck jump	3	5
Box jump	3	5
Lateral hurdle hops	2	5
Straight arm standing toss for height	3	8
Seated chest pass	4	5

Intermediate		
Exercise	**Sets**	**Reps**
Long jump toss	3	5
Static squat jump	4	5
High knee box jump	3	5
Straight arm backward overhead toss	3	5
Medicine ball chest pass	3	5

Advanced		
Exercise	**Sets**	**Reps**
Box to box jump	3	5
Forward chest pass	4	5
Depth jump and leap	3	5
Twisting sit up toss	4	5
Clap push-ups	4	5
Depth drop push-up	4	5

Volleyball

The goal of the volleyball program is to improve vertical jump and arm swing power. These programs are performed late in the pre-season phase of training, 2 days per week, and should be complemented with strength training and sport-specific anaerobic conditioning.

Beginner		
Exercise	**Sets**	**Reps**
Box landing	3	5
Tuck jump	3	5
Box jump	2	5
Ball slams	3	8
Overhead throw	4	5

Intermediate		
Exercise	**Sets**	**Reps**
Depth jump and side step	3	5
Static squat jump	4	5
High knee box jump	3	5
Rotational swings	3	5
Pullover toss	3	5

Advanced		
Exercise	**Sets**	**Reps**
Box to box jump	3	5
Hurdle jumps	4	5
Depth jump	3	5
Twisting sit up toss	4	5
One arm heavy bag push	4	5
Kneeling two-hand overhead throw	4	5

Basketball/Netball

The goal of the basketball/Netball program is to improve vertical jump and passing and shooting power. These programs are performed late in the pre-season phase of training, 2 days per week, and should be complemented with strength training and sport-specific anaerobic conditioning.

Beginner		
Exercise	**Sets**	**Reps**
Box landing	3	5
Tuck jump	3	5
Box jump	2	5
Medicine ball chest pass	3	8
Overhead throw	4	5
Finger rolls	3	5

Intermediate		
Exercise	**Sets**	**Reps**
Depth jump and sprint	3	5
Static squat jump	4	5
High knee box jump	3	5
Rotational swings	3	5
Pullover toss	3	5

Advanced		
Exercise	**Sets**	**Reps**
Box to box jump	3	5
Hurdle jumps	4	5
Depth jump	3	5
Twisting sit up toss	4	5
Rapid fire chest pass	4	5
Clap push-up	4	5

Rugby

The goal of the rugby plyometric program is to develop full-body power to improve power for all phases of the game. These programs are performed late in the pre-season phase of training, 2 days per week, and should be complemented with strength training and sport-specific anaerobic conditioning.

Beginner		
Exercise	**Sets**	**Reps**
Tuck jump	2	5
Box jump	3	5
Lateral hurdle hops	3	5
Straight arm standing toss for height	4	6
Seated chest pass	4	5

Intermediate		
Exercise	**Sets**	**Reps**
Long jump toss	3	5
Static squat jump	4	5
High knee box jump	3	5
Straight arm backward overhead toss	4	5
Medicine ball chest pass	3	5

Advanced		
Exercise	**Sets**	**Reps**
Box to box jump	4	5
Forward chest pass	4	5
Depth jump and leap	4	5
Twisting sit up toss	5	5
Underhand toss for height	4	5
Depth drop push-up	5	5

Field Hockey

The goal of the field hockey plyometric program is to develop lower body and trunk power. The lower body emphasis is on single-leg lateral and diagonal movements similar to the motions used in the running stride. The upper body emphasis is on rotational movements to build shot power. These programs are performed late in the pre-season phase of training, 2 days per week, and should be complemented with strength training and sport-specific anaerobic conditioning.

Beginner		
Exercise	**Sets**	**Reps**
Standing long jump	3	5
Lateral hurdle hops	3	5
Multidirectional hops	2	5
Seated trunk rotation	3	8
Twisting sit up toss	4	5

Intermediate		
Exercise	**Sets**	**Reps**
Alternate leg diagonal jump	3	5
Single leg hop	4	5
Lateral jump single-leg landing	3	5
Twist toss	3	5
Straight arm standing toss for height	3	5

Advanced		
Exercise	**Sets**	**Reps**
Single-leg lateral hop	3	5
Alternate leg push off	4	5
Single-leg long jump	3	5
Alternate leg lateral jump	4	5
Rotational swings	4	5
Hanging leg toss	4	5

Racquet Sports (Tennis, Badminton, Squash, Racquetball)

The goal of the racquet sports program is to improve lateral movement on the court and arm swing power. These programs are performed late in the pre-season phase of training, 2 days per week, and should be complemented with strength training and sport-specific anaerobic conditioning.

Beginner		
Exercise	**Sets**	**Reps**
Standing long jump	3	5
Lateral hurdle hops	3	5
Multidirectional hops	2	5
Seated trunk rotation	2	8
Twisting sit up toss	2	5
Reverse wrist toss	3	5

Intermediate		
Exercise	**Sets**	**Reps**
Alternate leg diagonal jump	3	5
Single-leg hop	4	5
Lateral jump single-leg landing	3	5
Twist toss	3	5
Straight arm standing toss for height	3	5
Overhead triceps toss	3	5

Advanced		
Exercise	**Sets**	**Reps**
Single-leg lateral hop	3	5
Alternate leg push off	4	5
Single-leg long jump	3	5
Alternate leg lateral jump	4	5
One arm heavy bag push	3	5
Side lateral toss	3	5
Bent lateral toss	3	5

Sprinting

The goal of the sprinting program is to improve explosive leg power and strength through the core. These programs are performed late in the pre-season phase of training, 2-3 days per week, and should be complemented with strength training and sport-specific anaerobic conditioning.

Beginner		
Exercise	**Sets**	**Reps**
Standing long jump	3	5
Rope jumps	3	5
Tuck Jump	2	5
V-up	4	5
Seated trunk rotation	3	5

Intermediate		
Exercise	**Sets**	**Reps**
Long jump toss	3	5
Single-leg hop	3	5
Underhand toss for height	3	5
Sit up toss	3	5
Straight arm standing toss for height	3	5
Overhead triceps toss	3	5

Advanced		
Exercise	**Sets**	**Reps**
Multiple long jumps	4	5
Repeat underhand toss for height	4	5
Speed box jumps	3	5
Push-off	3	5
Twisting sit up toss	3	5
Hanging leg toss	3	5
Leg throws	3	5

Boxing

The boxing program focuses primarily on trunk and upper body power to increase punching power. A secondary emphasis is on lateral lower body movements to help improve the leg drive when throwing punches.

Beginner		
Exercise	**Sets**	**Reps**
Standing long jump	3	5
Lateral hurdle hops	3	5
Multidirectional hops	2	5
Seated trunk rotation	3	8
Twisting sit up toss	3	5
Seated chest pass	3	5

Intermediate		
Exercise	**Sets**	**Reps**
Alternate leg diagonal jump	3	5
Single-leg hop	4	5
Lateral jump single-leg landing	3	5
Twist toss	3	5
Straight arm standing toss for height	3	5
Clap push-ups	3	5
Supine power drop	3	5

Advanced		
Exercise	**Sets**	**Reps**
Single-leg lateral hop	3	5
Alternate leg push off	4	5
Single-leg long jump	3	5
Alternate leg lateral jump	4	5
Rotational swings	4	5
Depth drop push ups	4	5
Rapid fire chest pass	4	5
Hanging leg toss	4	5

Soccer

The soccer program focuses on lower body power development to improve sprinting speed and acceleration. These programs are performed late in the pre-season phase of training, 2 days per week, and should be complemented with strength-training and sport-specific anaerobic conditioning.

Beginner		
Exercise	**Sets**	**Reps**
Standing long jump	3	5
Rope jumps	3	5
Tuck Jump	2	5
V-up	4	5
Seated trunk rotation	3	5
Overhead throw		

Intermediate		
Exercise	**Sets**	**Reps**
Long jump toss	3	5
Single leg hop	3	5
Underhand toss for height	3	5
Sit up toss	3	5
Soccer throw in	3	5
Overhead triceps toss	3	5

Advanced		
Exercise	**Sets**	**Reps**
Multiple long jumps	4	5
Repeat underhand toss for height	4	5
Speed box jumps	3	5
Push-off	3	5
Twisting sit up toss	3	5
Hanging leg toss	3	5
Leg throws	3	5
Kneeling two hand overhead throw	3	5
Two hand side throw	2	5

Photo & Illustration Credits

Coverdesign: Jens Vogelsang
Inside Photos: Ed McNeely & David Sandler
Cover Photo: dpa picture-alliance

IAAF
ATHLETICS
© IAAF 2000®